Love Letter from Luxembourg

New & Selected Poetry, 1998-2013

featuring
World War II Poems

John D. Thompson
FIRST EDITION, FIRST PRINTING

Copyright, 2013, John D. Thompson

ISBN: 9780972071765

LIBRARY OF CONGRESS CATALOG NUMBER: 2013910980

All Poems Written by John D. Thompson
Poetry Project Conceived by John D. Thompson

All rights reserved: no part of this publication may be
reproduced, stored in a retrieval system, or transmitted
in any form or by any means, electronic, mechanical,
photocopied, recorded, or otherwise
without written permission of John D. Thompson.

The poems may not be performed or translated
without the written permission of John D. Thompson.

Manufactured in the United States of America

COVER ART and GRAPHIC DESIGN by KARISA RUNKEL

VISIT, VIEW, and PURCHASE all books written by John D. Thompson at
www.facebook.com/PalindromePublishingOfIowa
Megan Williams, Site Manager

Palindrome Publishing of Iowa on CREATE SPACE
Pella, Iowa

E-mail author at: statepoetpro@yahoo.com
for book sales, signings, and readings.

for Ann

AUTHOR'S NOTE:

On January 3, 1945, Private First Class John D. Thompson
of the 345th Infantry Regiment, 87th Division, was killed in action
during World War II while serving his country, the United States of America,
at the Battle of the Bulge, in the Ardennes Forest of Belgium.
PFC Thompson was survived by his wife, Edith, and only child,
infant daughter, Ann. He was laid to rest at the Luxembourg American
Cemetery and Memorial.

The poet is named for the soldier.

Love Letter from Luxembourg

POEMS

NEW POEMS/MILITARY SET

Love Letter From Luxembourg	1
Draft	3
A Belgian Winter	4
Battle of the Bulge	5
Diphtheria	6
The Brooding of Mules	7
Miss the Missouri	8
Postage from Papa	9
To Burst Your Bubble	10
Twentieth-Century Penelope	11
Line of Duty	12
The Other Side of Salutation	13
Grief	14
A Hard-Knock Wife	15
Armed Forces	16
The Widow's Hour	17
World War Widow	18
The Limits	19
Sacrificial Hims	20
The Only Child Game in Town	21
Hatfield	22
Allendale	23
Paper Ghosts	24
Anne Frank of the Attic	25
The Kiss	26
Armistice	27
Public Domain	28
Swastika	29
Mourning	30
Battles	31
The Purple Heart	32
The Terms of War	33
Peculiar Weather	34
The World War II Veteran	35
The Dying Rate	36
Got a Name	37
A Second Kind of Coming	38
My Bicentennial Bedroom	39
She Can't Listen to Rock-and-Roll	40
Atavism	41
Mercy	42
An Eternity Overseas	43
Vessels	44
Ann for Each Anniversary	45
The Show-Me Scales	46

NEW POEMS / CIVILIAN SET

Rogaining for God	49
Ode to Vanity	50
The High Horse	51
Offending My Largesse	52
Caravaggio	53
Clifford Paul	54
The Eleventh of September	55
Put It to Ya'	56
Fraud	57
A Drowning Man	58
Munchausen by Proxy	59
It's My House	60
Thirteen Ways of Looking at the Shoes of Imelda Marcos	61
She Did, Too, Choke and Die in Bed with Pig	63
Ann Arbor	64
Scrimshaw	65
An Unkindness of Ravens	66
Audtioning for Monet's Garden	67
A Polite Rain	68
The Summer of '42 Retires	69
Living Among Our Assassins	70
Columbine	71

from *Hidden Voices from Hush-a-Bye Rooms*
1998

Black-Eyed Susan	75
Untouchable	77
Evergreen Revisited	78
Pioneer Woman	79
Border Town	81
Witness Non Grata	82
Scorpio	83
Artistic Jester	84
Outdoors Wanting In	85
Room Service for One	87
The AA Train	88

from *Prized Ponies*
2000

A Horse of a Different Color	91
Prized Ponies	92
Flow of Thought	93
The Twenty-Five Cent Horse	94
Cavalcade	95
Bluegrass	96
French Lick	97
Whippers & Trainers	98
Cantina Sestina	99
Breaker	101

from *Tender Revolutions*
2002

Kitchen Sink	105
Nuclear Family War	106
Chlamydia	107
Halfway Home	108
The Bell Curve	109
The Respired	110
Apria	111
Sadness Is a Place	112
ackity-ack-ack	113
The Scheming	114

from *Epiphany*
2004

Chapbook	117

from *99 Voices, 99 Lives: County Poems of Iowa*
2006

Plow in Oak, Oak in Plow: *An Audubon County Poem*	123
Portrait of Chief Black Hawk: *A Black Hawk County Poem*	124
Glow Depot: *A Boone County Poem*	125
Won't You Marry Me, Hill? Little Brown Church, Nashua: *A Chickasaw County Poem*	126
Among the Brome of Autumn: *A Decatur County Poem*	127
Hobo Convenience Store: *A Hancock County Poem*	129
Amity of the Amanas: *An Iowa County Poem*	130
The Smolder of Old Stone: *A Johnson County Poem*	131
Children of a Lesser Sod: *A Lyon County Poem*	132
Loess Hills: *A Monona County Poem*	133
Floppy Dish: *A Polk County Poem*	134
Letter from United Flight 232: *A Woodbury County Poem*	135

from *On Holiday*
2007

Cardinal Rules	139
Airing Christmas Laundry	140
Poor, Pitiful Pearl	141
Matchless	142
Nivea Campana	143
Elveswhere	144
The Skate at Scholte Gardens	145
Iceberg Rose, Greenwood Rose Garden, Des Moines	146
Albino Deer, St. Ansgar, Iowa	147
The Hierarchy of Angels	148
As on a Wintry Plain	149
Bethlehem, Pennsylvania	150
The Mother of Trees	151
The Snow Geese	152
I Am a Poor Boy, Too	153

from *Titanic: A Centenarian Voyage in Verse*
2011

Belfast Shipyard	157
The *Titanic* Stowaway	158
There Were Never Enough Lifeboats	159
Eastertide, 1912	160
God Himself Could Not Sink This Ship	161
The Iceberg Has a Word	162
Ticket to Survive	163
Dress Formal for Casualty	164
(Lying to) Women and Children First	165
Fifth Officer Harold Lowe's Blessing Those Without Boats	166
Isidor and Ida Straus	167
Rhymes with Ocean	168
Wallace Hartley, Leader of the Band	169
The Unsinkable Molly Brown	170
Jude Descending the Grand Staircase	171
Titanic Doll	172
Trolling for Bluefish	173
Sanding the Lifeboats	174
The Blue Period	175
The Revenant Ship	176
Dr. Robert Ballard Discovers the Hitherto Famous	177
A Partial Colossus	178

from *Iowa: A Place to Poem*
2013

Eastern Goldfinch	181
Old Geode	182
Land Between Two Rivers	183
Crinoid, Sea Lily	184
December 28, 1846	185
Trappistine Nuns and Caramels: Our Lady of the Mississippi Abbey	186
The Everly Brothers	187
Marian the Librarian	188
Cloris Leachman as Ruth Popper, *The Last Picture Show*	189
Dan Gable	190
Dewey Readmore Books	191
Monet at Brucemore Gardens, Cedar Rapids	192
Maquoketa Caves	193
Montauk, Governor Larrabee's Mansion, Clermont	194
Miss Havisham of the Meadows	195
Medusa at Gay Pride, East Village, Des Moines	196
The Cricket Waltz, Surf Ballroom, Clear Lake	197
Mother Goose at Fejervary Park Children's Zoo, Davenport	198
The Little Mermaid, Statue and Fountain, Kimballton	199
The Butter Cow, Iowa State Fair	200
Floyd of Rosedale	201
Rockford Sock Mittens	202
The Newspaper Iowa Depends Upon	203
Van Allen Belts	204
The Apostle of Wheat	205
Robert D. Ray, Governor or Iowa, 1969-1983	206
American Gothic House, Eldon	207
Hoover Birthplace, August 10, 1874, West Branch	208
Trees of Marcourt Lane	209
Provender	210
Native Prairie Fragment	211

Epilogue Poem

A Bluebird in Winter	213

Love Letter from Luxembourg   New & Selected Poetry, 1998-2013

Love Letter from Luxembourg

NEW POEMS

MILITARY SET

Love Letter from Luxembourg   New & Selected Poetry, 1998-2013

Love Letter from Luxembourg

Dear Ann,

From aerial view,
the country of Luxembourg, Grand Duchy,
looks like the biological heart,
unpretentious, without
symmetrical curves for the sake
of sentiment or art.

My own heart lies here—
undecorated, still—
in a coffin of Ardennes wood—
lies still, but remembers
that moment—*blitzkrieg* on my boot,
a land mine ignited
like a torched swastika—
before Commander cried, *Halt!*—
before the winter fox,
the mesmerized mind could decide otherwise.

For you, daughter,
the Second World War will be more
than a history lesson, an exam to pass;
it will be a heartless school, without recess,
a memory entombed,
family heirloom on the globe.
Spin, point to dame-teacher and speak knowingly—
Father died here.

Yes, it was Belgium where I died,
Battle of the Bulge,
killed and carried to Luxembourg.
Even a desperate, unforgiving war possesses its own bureaucracy.

I died in Belgium—
where the first casualty was beauty—
Belgium—where at best, the ends drew a sword's draw with the means.
In feverish bursts of blood,
we Americans signed away our lives in foreign snow.

Love Letter from Luxembourg

Love Letter from Luxembourg

I want you to know, Ann—
My boot did as it was told.
A soldier marches on—
Neither fool nor hero loses an appendage,
his life in step with an explosive destiny.
This was an act of an enlisted man,
your father on duty.
Perhaps I was holding a gun—
wishing elsewhere,
with you cradled in the last breath of my arms.

Ann, you will grow to surpass my years on Earth.
You have two Fathers in Heaven, and we will see to it.
From here, I can see to so many tasks,
each one a tour of love.
I see your extended family, stubborn and proud,
surrounding you like a blue body of closing, quiet water—
your children, my grandchildren, creating little wars of their own.

I live in the purple heart of the sky.
Consider me when you sing the word *home*.
Think of my fellow, fallen soldiers when you end the anthem with *brave*.
I am, at most, a cloud of brief sorrow.
This range, this pain, too shall pass.

It is said,
When looking for grace, gaze upward—
But my eyes look down, and there you are—
gracing the rocky breaks of Missouri, the grassy bends of Iowa
like the softest sparrow.

Each day, my angel wing,
I rise before you to offer the sun, this harp,
the tensions of the hour are merely strings for you to play.

I may be gone, but it's you who is on the go.

My Ann,
my soldier of infant swaddle,
my baby doll, our Show-Me girl,
the tiniest widow your world will ever know.

*—for Cousin Ann in memory of John D. Thompson, PFC
for whom the poet is named—*

Draft

With the draft
arrives a stiffening wind.

A ticket to war
cannons through air.

The gust of the moment enlists.
Brute reality is a breeze.

The letter effects
a chosen hand, steadily nervous,

for there is nothing more selective
than service.

A Belgian Winter

Blinding and beastly
With below-zero highs,
Its forest-freeze favors
Neither the Axis, nor the Allies.

Unseasonably cold,
Unreasonably cruel,
(It) petrifies fire
Makes a skate pond of fuel.

Beleaguering belligerents,
Frosting the francs,
It deadstops all tracks,
Even humbles the tanks.

Its ice knives through thickened sky.
Its sleet slits soldiers' throats.
The wool over their eyes,
Denser than the wool in their coats.

Battle of the Bulge

Cold confronts the woods of Ardennes,
seizes the trees in a deadlock of frigidity.

A break in the battle,
yet the weather is at war.

The snow is its own artillery,
firing blue-white bullets into the paralyzed exposures.

Fuel-hungry tanks immobilized, adrift—

The wind is a kind of tide;
it clears what it causes—

the moisture in a soldier's eye.

Diphtheria

It is both blanket and ice pick,
an envelope to coat
nose, throat, and bronchial tubes,
a mother of a membrane
suffocating a child of war in captivity's room—

then it transcends,
it becomes an intercontinental dart—

shooting its way across wide waters—
tapping the home front, door to door—
shattering the sill to the window
of the strong and the willed

until its cold tip enters the belief system
of the bereaved, and before it takes leave,

it breaks the heart.

—for Donald Eugene Luce
World War II casualty from Clarke County, Iowa

The Brooding of Mules

Packed as the congregate snows
besieging their assembly from brow to boot,
the American soldiers collect
alongside the flickering Ardennes timber sticks
and speak of faraway geographies—
the tobacco lanes of the Carolinas,
the infant casino ways of Vegas,
the industry hey-days stacked, a-line, the Great Lakes,
and the passage-plow brays of uncompromised Missouri.

Stubborn, they stand in their gray-dun coats,
white-muzzled, ear-alert, in case of true enemy confronts,
grunting, wind-down, of home-front comforts.

Careful not to cave,
suspicious of each other's whinny, lightest sigh,
this is the closest any of these gentleman beasts
to arrive at a true man's lullaby.

By morning,
the soft, white ammunition of clouds will pent up
a fortress, through which,
this barren of a battalion will levy a hoof-bounded road—
with strength of the horse,
sure-footedness of the jack,
fearless and frozen,
and like the mule itself,
calm, under the most cumbersome of loads.

—*for war veterans of northern Missouri and southern Iowa, Mule Country*

Miss the Missouri

When soldiers dream of home,
their reveries divide among geographies.

The West Coast enlisted
envision foam covering the coastline
like sugar frosting
and running, barefoot and boot-free,
with a sweetheart in a strapped one-piece
along the ripple-rhythms of being
released and free.

The East Coast arrivals
imagine they are clad in their service best
and head with their coiffed dates
for the shines of Broadway,
catching a first and last kiss
beneath welcome-home marquee.

The Midwest men of the military
actually miss chores,
the keeping of cattle,
the tending to grain,
whips of the wind against a horses' mane,

and they miss the way
the Missouri and the Mississippi,
two of the nation's mightiest rivers,
somehow work and exist together
for the good of the earth,

not like these two great powers overseas,
the Axis and Allies,
whose friction and fighting
strip the world of its worth.

Postage from Papa

Sticky, as the situation of war itself—
I lick the letter and transmit it to America, overseas—
Past the Jews in clandestine closets,
Over the corpses of Normandy.

As I, too, am confined to the bunker,
The words are confined to a single sheet,
Reduced in England to microfilm—
Inside a cargo ship for the States, the message's emissary.

Its destination is daughter Ann,
Warm in her winter crib, her infancy,
Her first season waiting for Santa.
I send her my love inside this Private's seal.

She, who is too young to read,
But never too young to feel.

To Burst Your Bubble

As other mothers shepherded their cherubs
To Sunday scriptures or daybreak mass,
Edith kept little Ann at home this Sabbath,
For ritual bath.

The foam, a kind of mote.
The child, a kind of spirited castle,
A princess in a lukewarm sea,
Novice mermaid roped to a soap
For sudsy travel.

Wash away Saturday's play,
The playground's stubborn dirt.
Wash away remnants of sleep,
And any residual hurt.

In a distant church basement, doughnut batter is frying.
In a faraway forest, up Belgium, battered soldiers are dying.

But not here—

Here, where the only hover is mother
Entrenched in lather and love,
Where the only mine is parental possession.
The lone bomb is the burst of a bubble
Among beaching-basin suds.

Sensitive, yes,
But, oh, so pleasing to the unified touch.

Twentieth–Century Penelope

Like Penelope,
in the epic sails
of the Greek hero Odysseus,
she waits at home, in Missouri, for her man,
waits and weaves a tapestry of *Taps,*
patterns of hope, reverence, and mourning,
dark and swan-like stitching, aquiline, dipping
curving for the vanished fastens of firm companion.

Time hangs on the wallpaper
like a sullen garland.
The room itself, Spartan, in its setting
of porcelain, patchwork, and baby.

Together, the coddled and courageous,
in the company of lonely.

There are few antiquities here,
no worshipful gods.

If there is thunder, lighting—
these accessories to storms are modest
and, with the rain, tend to the livestock and fields.

The bluest of lattice pies cools in the kitchen window.

She herself calms to a crust.
It is what the waiting do.

It is what the weaving must.

Line of Duty

In war,
it is the horizon
that is in first line of duty,
summoning the sunrise,
a sort of silent bugle cry,
pulling the world
out of the placid drifts of sleep,
preparing the fields
to fight.

The ears of the enlisted
awake to the alert hues.
Men assemble like pack dogs,
weapons fattened
for the requisite rounds of fire.

If anything stirs,
it is breath and precision,
a rhythmic focus,
forehead to fingers,
to channel and trace
the demarcations of the day.

The sky breaks, uneven.
Clouds form their entrenchments.

Whatever lines frame remaining hours
depend on accuracy
and a willingness to withstand angst.

In war,
the last line of duty is honor,
but, often, not until unspeakable horror
has its final say.

The Other Side of Salutation

Of all the sounds of war,
with its wounded words,
its abominable language
pounding the streets,
alarming the headlines,
gunning for civilian ears
like a triggered cadet,
the most vexatious din
rings softly within,
a tone wrenching each bone,
two words
sent inside a letter home,
the opening address, a deadly duet,
Deeply Regret.

Grief

Grief,
you breaking affliction,
you bereavement,
you care.

You swoop,
a desolate swan,
on my pond of despair.

You blade a hardy skate
across my stiffened soul.

You take a tear.
And you take a toll.

I dress for your dolor
in a scarf benumbing my neck.

And pale to a wither
amidst your wintry wreck.

A Hard-Knock Wife

In the matter of the mortal message,
a notice of death,
no one wants to be the long-shadowed receiver
beneath the darkened, open-door frame.
The soul longs to leave
with the quick, the wing-footed messenger—
helium-heeled, evanescent Mercury,
the courteous, consoling Hermes
who tips his cap,
then scurries to deliver the remains of the day.

These are heavy roses
refusing to be refused,
a box of candy wraps
where lingering bitter
separates from the sullied sweet.
Misery's spellbound moment—
a widow's lasting lament
invites itself into the house of wounds
to sit at the helm of hope, now tabled,
spreading its wares for the insufferable feast.

     —written at Kent & Clay's, Florida

Armed Forces

Soon after the letter from the State Department arrived,
formerly wived, freshly widowed
Edith found herself overlooking Ann's cradle.

One of her arms, its hand, gently clenching the railing—

Upon her shoulders came the call,
the bearing of other arms.

These are the arms of solace,
the arms of peace,
the arms of comfort in time of need.

These are the arms that lay themselves down
in knowing despair
as if they had tongues
whispering an incantation of prayer.

These are the arms of good friends and blood relatives,
the arms that tie, and the arms that bind.

These are the arms of silence.

And it is silence that sings the sweetest lullabies.

The Widow's Hour

It is she who is sedated,
tranquilized from interior terror.
The widow descends,
too much helium in her black balloon—
she succumbs among the willowy weeds,
catatonic to the claws
peer-popping about
for nocturnal feed.

The widow floats low in the wounded room.

She has digested the message from Europe,
inhaled the Army's winds of sympathy from Washington
sealed with an honorable dismiss.

Like time,
she is all hands and faces
with a ticker to tell her,
exhale—to take in—
how precious
even the pain is.

World War Widow

Global in her grief,
she sinks
through the nettlesome veil
of an exhilarating dawn,
its commanding propaganda,
stiffening her sobs
to acknowledge
the anguish of absence,
the bleaching glory
of gone.

The Limits

Somewhere,
near the tip of her wit
steeps a precipice,
the soul's border,
where all hope would leap

like a forlorn lover
into a gyring, color-of-coal abyss,
if she were to go there.

As much as she moves in sorrow;
more so, she must tread
with the caution
of an unwanted intruder.
Yes, her mind must step lightly over,
upon the breaking stones of grief.

If anything falls,
it is her ears, deaf,
to the summon-sound of sympathizers,
who inadverently call her to the edge…
when they speak,
Come to me.

Sacrificial Hims
American Military Cemetery, Luxembourg

In this amphitheater of the fallen,
cemetery for the soldier-dead,
stones of sacrifice align
as a convex community of crosses,
regimented requiem,
a pearl harbor of arching grace
along the light-lifting field.
A white anesthesia
spreads a calm ministry across
first fingers of morning
reaching, rising
as if the sky were an officer's temple,
and the stones were up for birdsong reveille
to exchange in reflective salute.

The Only Child Game in Town

The hand of cards
Life deals her
Spreads out like a fan of despair,
There, low-lying in infant-intent
Beneath the high-baby chair.
Come king, come queen.
Hither, club and spade.
Form your stocks and tableaus
In magnificent cascade.

She'll burp in her bib
When it's her turn to bid
Against herself, all odds, aside the crib
Amidst the ribbons and rhymes
Thresholds of thorned weapons and war crimes,
The rosiest of red-blood ruffles.
Nothing comforts the lack of company-content
Like the swaddle
Of the solitaire shuffle.

Hatfield

Being only three,
she believes Hatfield should be a place
where fedoras, bonnets, and derbies
rest on stems,
offering the faces of flowers there,
enough shade.

A tiny Alice herself,
she will be on the little-girl lookout
for any mad hatter,
a stranger to suggest a spot of tea.

Like the old barns and leaning porches around her,
time appears motionless,
undaunted even by the wind.

The word in that wind is that her own father
spent his boyhood summers here,
working and playing in these lidded fields,
growing strong with the feed cattle,
tall with the stretches of corn.

She imagines him in a Stetson,
triggering his finger like a play gun.
Then she sees her daddy as a headgear soldier,
trading in his artificial artillery for military's real McCoy.

As much as her minuet mind tries to respect it,
she wants her Daddy back, she wants her Pa.

She wants to play among these fresh fields
with that denim-strapped boy
fit and fancy-free in his handmade hat of straw.

Allendale

Softly,
as Ann and Edith approach
the memorial stone,
countryside,
near the small town
of Allendale, Missouri,
where John D.'s titles lie in tribute,
the sprits there
recognize that Ann
is without siblings,
a brotherless beauty
among sun-swept wildflowers of spring.

The cemetery itself, a meadow of mercy.

The deceased ancestors decide in unison
that its namesake shall split—
Allen to her left, Dale to her right,
each apparition holding a hand of Ann's,
guiding the girl through a sacred pasture
to the mark of her father.

As permanent and promised as the stone itself,
the town will be a set of soul brothers to her,
dutiful and dedicated to the preservation of a soldier's name,

escorting Ann each time she enters there
to light the memory of the eternal flame.

Paper Ghosts

Once she is able to speak,
Ann vows to collect paper ghosts
in lieu of paper dolls.

Her articulate hands will craft them
from images of sepia-toned photographs,
and she will hang them along invisible halls.

They will play open-heart house,
savor vaporous tea,
these fragile frames, thinly-linked, but strangely secure.

In time,
Ann will give these wraiths delicate wings,
but never firm feet…for they must never march off to war.

Anne Frank of the Attic

This is not the world I wanted,
a kind of sinister, simmering endurance
where the brush of a kitten
or tap of a porcelain cup
summons instant seizure,
eventual death.

I can change letters, sentences,
thoughts, whole pages,
but I cannot transform the war.

My mother is near me,
but I am far from her arms.

My family and the huddled others
live as a sort of one-celled creature,
unified fear, programmed effect,
confined to the cause of the Party.

We lie about the attic like trunks of old clothes.

I come here, not to the annex,
but to you, Diary, for refuge and sanctuary,
your bindings attuned,
open to original hope.

As routine as the hours are practiced and pass,
the atmosphere breaks each daylight, in silence,
to a disheartening divide.

Beyond the bookshelf downstairs,
there is a hissing.

I surmise it is either a tea kettle or spy.

The Kiss
V-J Day in Times Square, Photograph, 1945

If only the aftermath of war

were to remain like this,

the dame embraced,

a soldier kissed,

her pointed heel

in ecstatic pirouette,

when a war hero's lips

takes her purse of passion's nets,

her spine in suspended recline,

elegantly bent like a swan's neck,

whirlwind minds entwined.

If she were made of strings,

he'd pull from her clinging waist,

send her spinning

among the scatter-fly ticker tape.

If only this steam would never simmer,

this frame forever freeze

to capture this rapture

this flood of overjoy

that can only arrive

with service from overseas.

Armistice

Like the world itself,
the word *armistice* ends in *ice*,
after treacherous tongues
order subordinates to *fire*.

Death issues its doctrine
in a wintry breath
amidst broken bayonets—
what remains of the rest, eternal retire.

The contestable fields
harvest the fallen,
winnowed from reusable weapons,
their earthly dreams picked clean.

A quietude reports
to the official desk of darkness
where a final battle flickers—
between embers of sorrow and serene.

This is the hour of hush,
a muted landscape of mist
where strategic acts cease
to late-lunar howl of abandoned alarm.

A morning promise for peace arises,
but its frost-bitten fingers are crossed
because the polarized globe refuses
to lay downs its folded arms.

Public Domain

War,
like an old poem,
resides in the public domain—
exposed and exasperating,
it takes our lives,
our respirations away.

It makes its point.
It turns in its rooms.
It takes the sweepstakes,
for it is the broom.

It has literal intent
and figurative folly.
It hangs—hesitative— food for thought,
and funeral holly.

It creates old men
out of the spry ones, kiddo.

It dispirits the living.

It consoles the widow.

Swastika

Foursome of
            vile crows   Evil hinged
   dark regret   at wings
Quartet of   of Ravens   Third Reich

Mourning

It should suggest
the dawn of an encroaching day,

not digest
the fall of a decaying form.

It should revive
after requisite sleep,

not deviate
from the expected norm.

At best, it should crest
will all that fails.

At worst, it should descend
with all that broods and storms.

It is, after all, the knit-
stiching of dark veils.

It is, beyond nothing,
teary-eyed and torn.

Battles

From the time our fitful crusades
discharge us from escarpment of the womb
to the moment we wedge ourselves
into the ball turret of a fitted tomb,
we are engaged in battles.

We are enlisted in oxygen,
drafted by air,
winded by interior wars
whipping us like POWs into selective-service chairs.
We are engaged in battles.

In the heart of our own living rooms,
we feud overseas.
How strange this wave—
goodbye to first families.
We are engaged in battles.

We are summoned to the rank-and-file job force,
reasoned to serve in the military of motherhood,
retired with stripes and stars like derby horses
if the running was good.
We are engaged in battles.

We swear by the white cross of our hearts,
the blood streaming like banners from our falling heads
for the living republic,
for the union dead.
We are engaged in battles.

For warfare. For welfare.
The christened. The cursed.
The married. The marred.
For better. For worse.
We are engaged in battles

The personal. The political.
The mobile. The still.
This willing of want.
This wanting of will.
We are engaged in battles.

The Purple Heart

In technical terms,
It is a wall decoration.
From the emotional tongue,
It is anything but.
It murmurs in the minds
Of the left-behinds,
Beats upon the tightest skins,
Hangs in halls of fallen heroes,
Revives broken interiors
Of the weathered-within.

Its chambers palpitate
The veined strategies of war,
The chartered arteries
Of those who served,
Those who lie asunder
Eternity's hallowed mist.

It is the purpling plain,
A mountain majesty reign
Along Courage's shade-ranges
Plum, Orchid, Lavender, and Amethyst.

The Terms of War

Concentration is key.

It camps out on a Kristallnacht
to study the birth of blitzkrieg.

Blue-eyed sugar plums dance
upon Fuhrer's blonded brain.
Four-pronged swastika uncoils beastly limbs
on a Third-Reich sleeve.

And the world tilts
toward an evil Axis
until Allied boot prints
blanket the beaches of Normandy.

Arm chair, post-war conferences in Yalta, Potsdam—
from Manhattan, a bombs-away baby about to boom.

The student-soliders of war,
temporarily dismissed,
ere the cold calls of Korea
summon the guns back to the trench-desked rooms.

Four-star generals reap heroic apples.
Hitler hisses an exhale among the dirt-driven worms.

To arrive at the retrospective why of war,
you must first pause at because of the terms.

Peculiar Weather

Peculiar weather, we're having,
this struggle of war,
in like a lion
out like a roar,
cowardly and craven,
scare me,
what is for?...
a salute in my bugle-boots,
to its weather fronts,
whether it ends,
that's for the old ya-nay sayers
to score,
for war effort,
my heart
did its chambers-anger part,
believe me,
it   to re.

The World War II Veteran

The November wind ushers the gray parade.

Quartet of World War II veterans on Remembrance Day

March in orthopedic shoes, prescriptive ones

To a frugal bugle and diffident drum.

No media blitz to cover their pass.

Not a single school-aged child on field-trip from class.

The nation's emblems exhibit their hues

In accustomed patterns blood, pallor, and blue.

With senior-citizen synchronicity, they reminisce

The cheers of coming home, the hisses of Auschwitz.

Older than autumn, winter's approaching brothers,

They align arm-in-armistice with one another.

Decorated and bent like over-the-hill holiday trees,

These allies step with intent to preserve dignity.

In the palms of one, threadbare stars-and-stripes folded like a patriotic pillow,

The kind offered after the coffin is closed to the desolate widow.

Straight as a wrinkle, upright as a sag,

They who carried the country, now carry the flag.

The Dying Rate

A thousand of them are dying each day,
a new millennial sort of D-day,
with mortality combing ashore
the sandy beaches of a veteran sun.

Overpaid, over-sexed, and over here!
The British once bemused about their Allies.
Overage, overtime, an overture
plays to the deaf, techo-obsessed nation

they were designed to protect.

These are the original angry birds,
parachuting like portentous limbed bombs
behind enemy lines, the American hero
blazoned, once again, across a world-wide sky.

Hemispherically theatrical, impregnably impractical,
they dismantled the swastika,
leaving Hitler with sorrow's bluest eyes
beneath a dumb-blonde, ashen grave.

They are crumbling like the Berlin Wall,
but only in bone, to register for the After Draft.
Their ticker-tape hearts pour over and out
one last passing parade,

a waving grace of goodbye
to a world they freed, a globe they saved.

-for the World War II Veteran
-inspired by John Busbee

Got a Name

In 1973, ABC Records released
an album and song of the same title,
I Got a Name by folk/pop singer Jim Croce.

It was a posthumous issue.

Croce had died, late summer, in a plane crash
just days before these namesake recordings
hit the charts.

Among the spirited lyrics are similes
drawing his name to the pine trees lining a road,
singing birds, northern winds, and croaking toads.

The music is hauntingly biographical to me.

I, too, have a name—
a posthumous release.

I carry it with me like my father's brother did.

It is prize. It is pride. It is possession.

Leaving it in signature all these years has been my one art.

It is the anthem causing me to rise each morning.

It is the voice on this page.

It is the hand over my heart.

A Second Kind of Coming

We study it in the Last Testament,
a parting promise of *Revelation*.

He is coming with the clouds.

But what if it never will happen
because it is happening now?

What if it is not promise, but process?

What if it lives in dreams and rests in daylight?

What if it is breath to all our labors?

What if among the evil, terror, and horror—

it is the one true endurance and favor?

What if it is spectrum of our emotions, the arc of cries and laughter?

What if its evidence is not, so much, in being born again

as it is in the naming after?

My Bicentennial Bedroom

I am named for a man,
a soldier, my uncle
whose boot stepped
on a field mine
while fighting
the Battle of the Bulge.

And so,
I spent my boyhood
in a room of red, white, and blue
where steel eagles with talons of iron
and drums carved out of Avon soaps-on-a-string
fastened themselves to my interiors.

A room plastered and postered
with silver-dollar patriotism—
the fifty states, their capitols,
symbols of bird and flower—
and, of course, portraits of presidents
watching over me like godfathers.

It is no revolutionary thought
that a poet is not a fighter,
and, sometimes, I think—
a poet is not a man
as I remember that childhood
in my bicentennial bedroom

where the only battle
was how to handle homework
and the only bulge
was the sifting of pillows
among the many comforts
my parents provided me.

She Can't Listen to Rock-n-Roll

Who is to assume my place, the fatherly hold?
Who will chase the fly-boys from our dim-lit porch?
Who will tell Ann she can't listen to rock-n-roll?

Who will guide her hand down each rhythmic road?
Who will light her blindness, carry the first torch?
Who is to assume my place, the fatherly hold?

Who can further craft this art, dearest daughter from my mold?
Who will separate the beats, when the blue sounds and black fury forge?
Who will tell my Ann she cannot listen to rock-n-roll?

Who will teach her to twirl to the big bands, in spins of gold?
Who will show her the stage where the brass blow like winds of true north?
Who is to assume my place, the fatherly hold?

Who will keep her on the up-and-up, away from the down low?
Who will set her to swing music, send her marching forth?
Who will tell my Ann she cannot listen to rock-n-roll?

Who will suggest to her Elvis is a passing fad, the Beatles a band soon old?
Who will give her the thrill of Miller, the Mills Brothers, Goodman, Bing and his sort?
Who is to assume my place, the fatherly hold?
Who will tell Ann she can't listen to rock-n-roll?

Atavism

It is said that, occasionally, descendants,
distant relatives skimming through family albums,
discover an old photograph of the deceased
pressed like a promenade orchid,
tinged in sienna shades of light,
chafed around broken-crust edges—
yes, among these buried flashbulbs of the past,
they unearth a staggering, stately image
that is the spit-shine replica
of a loved one, currently living.

Something in the cut of the jaw,
or gleam of an eye,
or break of a hairline,
or perhaps a myriad of traits—
yes, something, about the present moment
reverts to the ancestral hour.

The discovery, at first, dilates the pupils,
quiets the tongue, like bearing witness to a ghost,
who has paused for an intimate portrait.

And you begin to believe in gifts
that only your bloodline can open,
miracles only biological souls can share.

You start to understand,
in the clearest black and white,
the heavens take and leave us,
the skies accept and deny.

And somewhere in their sense and mystery,
the old adages ring both false and true.

You cannot come back, because you never left.
And because you never left,

you can't take it with you.

Mercy

Like a twig of lilac or ripening fruit,
it thrives in mist.

It follows the tear like a loyal hound.

It is the color of the cross at Eastertide,
and contains itself with the elegance
of a dove at repose.

You call to it, *Mother.*
You cry to it, *Mary.*

It is there with a *there, there*
when the wounds are open
and hope is closed.

It appears with the quietest whimper.
It knows your soul is wet, and the heart damp.

Unselfish and shameless, it bares itself before you.
Permits you to morph it into shawl or shroud.

It commits to your hour of sorrow.
And in mere minutes, it is your oldest friend.

Whatever the matter—will pass, will pass.

And so its company ends.

It was there for the disbelieving.
It was there to collect your grief.

And like a well-mannered guest,
it knew it best,
when you summoned the strength
to request that it leave.

An Eternity Overseas

A revered poet once wrote
you could hold eternity in an hour,
see the world in a grain of sand.

He was wrong about that.

Oh, an eternity, the world for that matter, may begin
with the stuff beach castles are made of—
but, like Charybdis, that great mythical pool,
it swallows all crafted sails whole.

An eternity can neither be held nor seen.
An eternity must be spent.

And it is no pocket change
for your pleasure and pain.

Eternity is perpetual rent.

You can pay by the chamber or room,
charter its rollicking cruise,
but do not equate it with time—
expect neither a tangible shoreline,
nor land-ho horizon to unfold.

No, you cannot share eternity
with a grain of sand in the palm of your hand.

You must spend it
with the stones anchored in your soul.

Vessels

If you believe in anything,
believe in vessels,
ships of the whisper,
boats of abundant blessings,
come-again cargo,
gifts from God's inexplicable sea.

Believe in the message of the bottle,
folded and tucked
inside the body of a blood-relative boy,
purpose and plan,
the wave and wand of His invisible hand—
the time and tides that carry you to me.

Ann for Each Anniversary

Thank God for the infant

Thank God for the child

The neonate too new for memory

The just-born too coddled for the world's wiles

Thank God for the innocent

Thank God for the new

The pretty in pink

Who brings hope in fresh hue

The Show-Me Scales

Ann,
Show me *A* is for *apple*.

Baby,
Show me *B* is for *blue*.

Cuddle,
Show me *C* is for *cat*.

And at *D*,
Daddy holds a *doll* waiting to be held by you.

My lovely,
Live your life to the letter.

E for *earth* angel, *F* for her angel's *face*

And at *G*
Show me the gift God gave to you.

Ann, show the world your *grace*.

NEW POEMS

CIVILIAN SET

Rogaining for God

I, too, apply it—
formula of faith,
diurnal ritual,
bare necessity.

It is solution, appeasement,
hope-against-hope orison
for the neat extinct fur algae,
now beneath see-level,
once indigenous to my
arctic skull.

It is supplement for my supplication
to that Cosmetologist in the Cosmos.

Among the oldest population in the country,
I, too, am aging,
slowly buying the farm,
while on my knees in prayer—for hair.

The Lord is listening,
looking down at yet another polar cap,
another receding canvass of global change.

He is lachrymose & He cries
into the eye droplet,
brunette baptismal, cosmetic anointment,
eternal remedy for the chronic monk's tonsure.

I walk from the Great Basin
& *raspberry* to the sky
the infernal infidel, sooty angel,
yes, that filthy flake
who left the cigar burn there,
instead of my hair, in the first place—
a singe, a sin
for God & all of smoke-free heaven to see.

Ode to Vanity

Vanity, you flaming fair,
you feathered romp, you pomp parade
your sense of self
you shadowed wall
always up for a game
of charades

one word, three syllables
sounds like *sanity*
point conveyed

pensive as an egotist
contemplating faded days

Vanity, I
reflect, genuflect
to you—
or is it I—
so ablaze
once upon the mirrored—page—
and you as I
will be anyone
do anything

but age

The High Horse

Dreaming He's Greek again, a fresh-lush God
bred from the right wing of Pegasus,
The High Horse is the other Mount Olympus—
His saddle of braided-brush sage
tacks on the cloud-range crested.
A rider of the soprano sky,
He teethes the bridle gold,
each stirrup, a silver spoon.
The boost-beast fingers and bites silly,
sacrificial limbs looking in His cubed-sugar pout.

Bucking the gadfly,
leaving mortals to find their own damn way home,
the patrician pony takes out on His own
to where air and blood are rarefied blue.
The sun in the star-gazed pasture,
a mere footman preparing the Tall Stall.
Only angels in training wings are above Him.
Even they bow to His ascension in unison
of exasperating, ethereal *O's*—
The Chrysos crown donned upon Him
to golden rule the soaring, perpetual bright-night.

But haste precipitates in royal firmament;
Swift cirri darken with waking of Schadenfreude's delight

as the rain,

both reins,

His reign

begins to fall.

Offending My Largesse

The needy of the world are offending my largesse.
I offered them my gifts.
I shared to all my blessings.
I suffered for each victory,
I even thrived in occasional defeat,
Only to realize,
The world
One thing
Without me—

complete.

Caravaggio

Boys of the bare shoulder
gather their poses and go down
the supine throat of his storied flat.

Merisi, the last Michelangelo, is alone in his studio
& eye-level with the unsuspecting pedestrians of Caravaggio;
the city will surrender its name to this resident artist
to avoid confusion with the chiseler of David.

The quick oils on each canvass compete in a dry run
to divert his attention from sodomy, self-obloquy.
The first one finished hangs itself; the Spartan-clad others follow suit
& hammer themselves in the light-slanted hall—
erect nails, each the size of a moppet's neck.
At last one, still fresh, throws its indecency at his manifest indifference.

His palate drips elsewhere, outside,
among the mundane wages of provincial Bergamo,
where a wet Saturday scurries the same male slatterns
to awnings of questionable position.

He paints them again from the loft of memory—
nascent faces, prepubescent places—
without a stripling's consent—
little lords immortalized by the balding hairs of his brush.

The room is a mind in a hurry, but his tongue is in no rush
to share with the peripatetic citizenry his custodial desire
connecting clandestine dots, exterior to interior, *brother to brothel.*

Malestro strokes the last piece with a chiaroscurist's penchant for gray borders
& leaves himself in the eclectic company of still-shadow fruit, silhouette roses,
his own sexual Jesus, & regalia genitalia of immodest saints.

Some will die on the cross of his unexamined imagination.
Some will escape via tossed fly-water jar or flung newspaper vase.
What suspects remain speak through their wings.

Their fleeting formality forgives his Mannerist digressions;
murderous self-confessions
& strong-breath suggests a single imperative: *paint.*

Clifford Paul

My father's name was Cliff,
but it was I who took him to the edge;

over the precipice we'd go
beneath the undertow

ripping to foam-remnants
the flotsam of our souls.

Cigarette Sunday drive,
our lungs entwined for a dive,

we'd argue like battering swans
flapping elongated wings like steak knives

good for eating the crossbreds he killed,
but not for keeping a bull-calf relationship

alive.

The Eleventh of September

September—

And the sky is wearing

White airplanes after Labor Day.

A good morning in good America

Witnesses the fashion faux pas

Clashing into towers of world trade.

One, say two, false steps for mankind.

Pigeons stop their later-summer lovemaking.

A firefighter from the Bronx

Drops his egg/mayo sandwich

To become a six-inch television screen hero.

And the Ground known

For boroughing such staggering numbers

Is Zero.

Put It to Ya'

I cannot fall with George, wouldn't wash with me.
I could lie about a cherry tree.
I've no axe to grind, just let me put it to ya'.
Swear upon these teeth of twigs,
it was the other guy in clouds of wig.
(Besides, Mom could use a bowl for pies;
so, Earth, cut a piece of crust, pie-wide;
& let a bald-faced baker put it to ya'.)
Put it to ya', put it to ya'.

A Dixon woman, a close-knit war
knows the postman's boots at ten o' four.
A Mason's heel at porch, *Belle, let me put it to ya'*.
Her parlor divided between living & lavender hearts—
a father, son, holy union seceded, blown apart.
Lincoln splits another rail, sends his regards.
Open the letter, ma'am, swallow hard
& let the blue-gray bruise put it to ya'.
Put it to ya', put it to ya'.

America roars in the Twenties, she can & she kicks.
Wall Street records, reports felicitous hits.
The ticker tapers, *Better sit down, kids; how do I put it to ya'*.
Thank you for coming, good times, transient guest.
That's a-nay to going back home, even the horse is depressed.
Peel me a grape of wrath.
Lay the remains upon Rose of Sharon's breast,
Let the resign of the times put it to ya'.
Put it to ya', put it to ya'.

A withered man in a withered age
tests up-HIV, waits for AIDS.
If only his brain could name who paid to put it to ya'.
He is ribbed as a rail, twigs on a tree.
There lies the door of life fumbling for its key.
Here swings cold & broken hinge.
Bend over, bare ass for the cocktail-syringe
& let post-modern science try to put it to ya'.
Put it to ya', put it to ya'.

Hallelujah.

Fraud

It, too, crawls,
creeps on little feet—
one for serpentine saunter,
another for deceit's dance,
light two steps
a thin mist over
consumer's view
of hope's harbor,
coys city suckers
a Cheshire wink—
foggy, but firm
in willowy stance.

Only fat thing about it is chance.

A Drowning Man

It is his failure to accept—
It is acceptable to fail—
That causes the waves around him to rise
And those salt-stung arms to flail.

Buoyed only by a boat-load of his blunders,
Immersed within a flotilla of flaws,
He will snatch at anything suggesting it can swim,
He will clutch at any proverbial straw.

Anchored by an iron will to stroke his addictions,
He seizes key loved ones about him; together, they sink like a Strauss.
Ashore, all accounts of them, sapped and drained;
Below, this blue misconstrue, not a dry eye in the bathhouse.

Munchausen by Proxy

My mother makes me sick.
She stocks up on noodled soups in the clandestine pantry.
Sloping on the sofa,
I, her infirmed, prepare for the winter games.

Coach and judge for the tedious, terrifying events,
the self-appointed nurse examines a team of index cards
lining the olive recipe file
and explores like a surgical veteran for

Blood Basted in Urine—
How to Taint a Petri Dish—
among the notes of medical history
she and I are making.

Giving her fever,
I wallpaper my room with the degrees
of dethroned doctors—suspicious twits released
to make way for her *MD—Maternal Diagnosis.*

I open wide for seasonal necessity,
a time for care and giving, factitious fairytale.
She is Winkin', Science is Blinkin'.
All I have to do is nod.

It's My House

Come to my porch, Breath-of-Suffer.
Resuscitate near death, this desire—
the loss, not of losing,
but letting go.

The silver leaf chilled
knows the white dust on the branch
bears the long tooth of winter.
Lovely, how lovely, the rooted grow old.

In the cellar, dank stupor,
sealed fruits of the forsaken—
Hands of lament let the rope
to the Underworld's core.

Come, Breath-for-Another.
To desire is to suffer.
The knock is not hard
until you open the door.

Thirteen Ways of Looking at the Shoes of Imelda Marcos

I.
Among twenty walk-in closets,
the only moving thing was the espadrilles
as she fled the castle.

II.
I was of three kinds:
Ferragamo, Givenchy, Chanel
in which there are three soles.

III.
The shoes whirled in autumnal rebellion.
It was a small part of the populist pantomime.

IV.
A president and his first lady
are one.
A president, his first lady, and her shoe collection of 3000
are one.

V.
I do not know which I prefer,
the beauty on the top shelf
or the beauty of those still in boxes,
the shoes horning
or just slipping-on.

VI.
Salesmen from Payless filled the estate lawn
with barbaric pitches.
The shadow of shoes past
crossed the lines to and fro.
The mood
laced in aglet & shadow—
an undeniable, untiable cause.

Thirteen Ways of Looking at the Shoes of Imelda Marcos

Thirteen Ways of Looking at the Shoes of Imelda Marcos

VII.
O thin men and women of Quezon,
why do you imagine golden strings?
Do you knot see how the Shoe Empress
in-steps around the feet
of the poverty about you?

VIII.
I know how to accessorize, accent
lucid, inescapable color coordinates;
but I know, too,
that Imelda is involved
in what I know.

IX.
When the re-election eschewed out of sight,
it marked the edge
of the shoes' outlines and the end of the social circle's shopping season.

X.
At the sight of shoes
flying past the police car lights,
even the whores and sailors with hands caked in Manila waivers
would cry out like harpies.

XI.
Ferdinand rode over Marikina
in a glass slipper.
Once, an ear of conscience pierced him,
in that he mistook
the shadow of her last dress
for 8 ½" rubbers.

XII.
The boat in the South China Sea is moving.
The sales receipts must be sinking.

XIII.
It was evening all of 1986.
It was snowing justice,
and it was going to snow for the heart of Corazon.
Imelda and her footmen sat
in the shoe trees.

After Wallace Stevens' *Thirteen Ways of Looking at a Blackbird*

She Did, Too, Choke and Die in Bed with Pig
July 29, 1974—England—Cass Elliott dies of a heart attack,
a deli sandwich rumored to be at her side.

All of Hollywood and Hippiedom hate
the fact that a slab of ham cut her voice,
stole Mama's thunder without Heimlich, choice.
The perils of Greece knew much kinder fates.
For God's sakes, Cass—snacks in bed?—sit up straight!
When London hog fogs your pipe, toot some noise—
or just drink some water, milk, swallow moist.
Hold the mustard, mayo, and clean your plate!

At the funeral, all the grief was brown
and the ties were gray like deeply charred meat.
I stopped in the church; Preacher served pate'.
California, half-mast, a Higher Ground
reaping stoned minds, throats hacking in spewed seats.
What Christ can't save, sandwiched phlegm takes away.

Ann Arbor

Like a spectral
forest of one,
a tree shows
through a woman's
buttermilk dress
of old paint.

Carved on
its crusted trunk,
the original artist's signature—

Intent

Scrimshaw

Who and from where are we—
If not by both of land and sea

It is not the writing on the land-locked wall, I tell you.

It is the hieroglyphics of the sea,
Accords of ancestors drowning
In the inaugural attempts of marine mercantilism
That keeps the abysmal man afloat.

It is not the scripting in the bottle,
But these cryptic pictures of fledgling ships
On broken tusks of blue-elephant fish,
That tell-tell the heart of the whale hunter,
What speared his journey,
The wading bird's vane guidance,
Heroic deeds archived on the pictographic lists.

It is not the mermaid's dictation on the embarrassed faces
Of coral caught in the act of creation
That log the tide's nocturnal business,
But the transcendence of these fin-carved,
Opaque jewels through the flensing of breath
And the piracy of fools that will decode
The tangle of weeds submerging us in leagues of mystery,
Prune Neptune's overgrowth, get to the salt of our aquatic-hooked history,
As we sit beneath the lighthouse farthest starboard on the cape
And decipher our destinies on waning foreheads
How as mammals we hardened like wax-museum features
On the real estate of such fixated, sanded stools.

An Unkindness of Ravens

Edgar,

I believe
The wounded shore has wings
Over battered waters
Leave
An unkindness of ravens

Vincent,

Grieve, dear,
Lend fell stars an ear
Winter wheat season
Tears
An unkindness of ravens

Ms. Sexton,

Stay home
Bake your pies, not poems
Crust your talents
From
An unkindness of ravens

Artistry,

Mind fire
Jade jackets hunt your hour
Bang-bang blackberry skies
Shower
An unkindness of ravens

NOTE: The poem is an invention termed **A Quintet Address,** *directly spoken, 5-line stanzas, variant word count, 2-5-3-1-4: Edgar Allan Poe, Vincent Van Gogh, Anne Sexton, and Artistry.*

Auditioning for Monet's Garden

Welcome to Giverny, you budding aspirants!
A flower's papers must be in order.
The resume'—water tight—with a reflective quality.
Patience is a requisite outside the high stone wall.
Naturally, both Monet the man and artist must favor you.
Now, let's see—can you work in spring or do you prefer autumn?
Don't fuss with a card or sack of seedlings.
If he wants to hear from you, we'll call.

Are you familiar with triangulation?
Color, perspective, and symmetry—
How you petal your wares against others?
Any allergies to flora, ecstasy, or fame?
The Garden speaks in languages Japanese and French. Do you?
Could you possibly learn abruptly upon appointment?

Quickly, I need plants A through M to follow me—
Aubretias to magnolia daisies.
Come, fleet-of-leaf, as instructed in the Clos Normand.
We will further divide upon brute inspection—
The arid from the aquatic, recherche' from the common.
Azaleas and lilies, continue immediately to the basin-pond.

I must ask you all to remain silent.
Shoo away, you shutter bugs!
No photographs beyond this point.
After all, all lasting impressions will be made by Monet.
When he appears with his palette, gaze into his facade for count of three,
Then dig deeply into the sod.
Oh, by the way, never, ever call him *Claude*.
Au revoir and shams of four-pronged clover!
A tip from one who has stilled for this practice-portrait—
The secret is not how well you look in pink roughcast tones,
But before the eyes of God.

A Polite Rain

Permission to pour?
inquires the sky at breakfast.
Its kettle of condensation
unable to keep
the morning brew back.

Why, of course!
my dry retort.

For when my brick throat
& slick coat are thirsty,
I like my clouds like my coffee—

thicker, billowing, & black.

The Summer of '42 Retires

Swift summer is blessed;
her hour knows.
She slims her skin
of winter's robes.

Her moons are brief;
the sun breathes long,
smoothes the scales
of Pisces' song.

From spring ides
her rise, an aqua bloom—
petals of heather
steal me to her summer room.

June's fire flies
& August hides
to skirt the heat—
July's entwine.

The autumn flowers;
September leaves.
Our solstice, love, suits itself
in shawls of listless, linen memories.

An earth-tone vest,
one of us dressed
for fall.

Living Among Our Assassins

If anyone has tried, conspired to kill you,
then you know paranoia is mere water
on the shoal, compared to blood cooking
beneath your rival's obsessed skin.

You borrow a breath belonging to all and ask,
Did I live?

Any dick-for-a-dollar can execute the contract
for a loaded man.

Ten-thousand *chee*$e will terminate an enemy
to eternal knees in most U. S. cities.
You can't bury the kindred for that.

Some of us live among those who could just kill us.

Vengeance, superiority, entitlement—
the possible motives line up
under suspicious lights—
abstract as abdominal instinct.

And who is your assassin, but someone
who took from this world?
He or she did!
Not just your soul but getaway gasoline,
fresh newspaper, fresh patch of knoll grass,
Eden's rib.

Still, we rise and walk the hour
to the chance of crossing our own Calvary
among blades, bullets, and beasts—
the personal, political—designed to do us in.

Indeed, paranoia is just water skinning the surface;
the knife in your dorsal portal, the fin.

Columbine

April 20, 1999

I was savoring lunch time,
Quick bread, a half of an hour
The girl to my right said, *Columbine*
Meant a perennial mountain flower

It grew, early summer, like a rocket of red swans
Rising, unlike wisteria, with a shoot of green earth
A prayer of color, a splash of charisma
From God's modest dirt

I was savoring our last time
Brief breath of the children's hour
The boy to my left slumped like a bent stem
During the artillery shower

It grew, early spring, like a rocket of blood bombs
Rising, high-school hysteria, the cafeteria, its own line of fire
Twelve classmates, two murderers, one teacher dead
And a nation lying upon a student-body funeral pyre

from

Hidden Voices from Hush-a-Bye Rooms

1998

Black-Eyed Susan

My feet have never broken the soil of India
My eyes are not native descendants of Amerigo Vespucci
I am the daughter of an unknown tribal man
Generically classified as an Indian
Politically refined as a Native American
I am the surviving member of a vanished clan

Black-Eyed Susan was my name
Though I could not keep it
I was born along the Trail of Tears
Like the wind
My father rose only to die
I buried the rhythm by his side
Where it has remained dormant
For one-hundred years

Without my father
Denied my mother
I left the badlands of Oklahoma
For the banks of a northern shore
A White trader from Missouri claimed me
The voices of my conscience blamed me
As Black-Eyed became Susan Eleanor

That was the last I saw of the wind and the rhythm
As I entered a world so foreign and dark
I played the role of society's captive
To mirror the shadows seizing my wild heart
And it was my heart's own remorse
Running like a team of untamed horses
Striding in vain to catch a whisper
Of my family's faded cry
Unable to keep pace
Absorbed by some holy human race
Susan Eleanor lay Black-Eyed Susan down to die

Black-Eyed Susan

Black-Eyed Susan

Now, I am an old woman returning
A century out of style
Capitalism and computers
Concrete stretches
Where my unscathed spirit once roamed for miles

The call of confusion abounds
As the language is awkwardly passed around
From one acceptable term to another
Drawing blood from my veins
The Bureau of Indian Affairs attempts to legalize
Something no Awareness Month will ever realize
I was your sister, and now I am your brother

When my ancestral flesh-and-blood discovered
A photograph of me last summer
Those ancient rhythms revived to dance
The orphaned wind caressed my sleep last evening
I close my eyes and dream of the chance
Of wandering down to the banks of the forgotten river
Leaving my civilized clothes on the shore
I immerse the souls of Susan Eleanor and John
And emerge as Black-Eyed Susan once more

Alongside the gentle clap of waters,
A legacy of lost people awaits to embrace me
As we speak in silent tongues
We are old in nothing but wisdom
The untouched world around us is young

My feet have never broken the soil of India
My eyes are not native descendants of Amerigo Vespucci
I am the daughter of an unknown tribal man

*—paternal grandmother of the poet,
several generations*

Untouchable

Beware of the storefront of my smile
The façade on my face
Legions of lesions and lovers
Hidden in place
A face full of promises swept away in the past
As I descend the stairway from heaven
To join the ranks of an ascribed lower caste

The millennium has mistreated me for so long
The century has cheated me so wrong
As if I were born

Untouchable

Withdrawn in shame and silence
A soul shattered apart
My fingers reach down among the ruins
To strangle my heart
A face full of promises
Once basking in light
Masked by the Black Plague who seduced me one night

The millennium has mistreated me for so long
The century has cheated me so wrong
As if I were born

Untouchable

I am a harvest-moon flower in autumn's chilling hour
My leper-like leaves are untouchable
I am thunder of meekness, the wonder of weakness
My bludgeoned spirit believes this
I need no passing prayers, no lullabies good night
I need the miracle cure of love
To restore the morning of my life
Oh, how I feel this

A harvest-moon flower, autumn's chilling hour
Leper-like leaves

Untouchable   *—for victims of HIV/AIDS*

Evergreen Revisited
Written for my parents' 40th Anniversary

Love,
Time's masterpiece of painstaking care
Love
In need of an artist's gentle flair
A portrait of a family
Underneath the sky's canvass of blue
I have hand-painted
With you

As an infant rose
Weathering the season's storm
I bore petals of optimism
Love would mature and warm
Love,
Ye Old English Inn
Cozy and clean
A vacancy for two

Your and I draw wells of water
From thirst
We reap food for thought
From mindless hunger
The sun will rise beaming rays of praise
Along the universe
Hands rush to applaud us
For we possess a picture-perfect love

Where two hands join as one
Infinitely wrapped around each other
When the day is done
Hours of devotion
Soft-spoken, pledging our love
Towers of emotion
Never rising above
The height of one love
Effortless endeavor
Forty years and forever
Green

Pioneer Woman

Turn back at the turnpike sign
Ignore the concrete and machine-painted lines
Walk down an abandoned country road
Beyond the last tilled acre
Lies the untouched soil of our Divine Maker
Heaven waits for those who go

The urbanite is unable to divide
The heritage humming in the mind
From the wild, rolling prairie
Where a man with pith
Bloomed into a legendary myth
Depending upon whom he married

The pioneer man shouted to his pioneer woman,
The land is free!
Whispering under his buried breath,
…but it will cost your life…

The portrait of my great-grandmother on the wall
Her forlorn expression tells it all
A smile forced so consciously
The bruises on her face and hands
Like a monumental brand
Of her destiny
Her message through me crawls
Modern man cannot comprehend the call
She remains a mystery

Who were the homestead brides
Who were the pioneer women and wives
History does not seem to know
Nobody bothered to write
Their tales of toil and sacrifice
Their legacy with the Old West wind blows
…the land was free, but it cost her life…

Pioneer Woman

Pioneer Woman

In her lover's lust for land
She nothing more than a helping hand
Granted no deed or mind of peace
A flock of frontier plans
She, the sacrificial lamb
Sheared of her fleece

In letters sent back East
Her city sisters, they would grieve as they would read
Accounts of loneliness, sorrow, gross neglect, and greed
Messages of loneliness, sorrow, gross neglect, and greed
A life of loneliness, sorrow, gross neglect, and greed

Border Town

Lamoni, Iowa

I am a border town near the Show-Me State
No mountains' majesty, no amber waves of grain
I am centuries from my ancestors
My years are bookends between my days

I am the last chance stop for half an hour
If you're northbound on 35
I am the memory left far behind you
Yet in spirit I remain alive

I am an apple orchard in November
Fresh produce from a roadside stand
I am your mama's first and last wake-up call
I am your daddy's calloused hand

I am Liberty Hall and Graceland
Standing sentinel as I stood decades before
I have no key or keyhole
I am an eternal open door

I am those newborn and those deceased
I am those who raised and those who bereaved them
I am the dreams you dare to dream
I am the reason, you claim, you cannot achieve them

I am a border town.

I am the spring photograph of your eldest daughter
In her hand-sewn formal gown
I am the tears falling with the leaves next autumn
When that young woman heads, forever city-bound

I am a livestock sale on Thursday
Quilts preserve me in my old age
For some, I am one last breath of freedom
For others, my boundaries are a lifelong cage

I was born and bred Middle American
Look closely, I am a sampling of the South
I hide behind two interstate signs, a stone's throw from a rural route
I am town…Where you are bound…Wherever you are bound

Witness Non Grata

Quarantine the witness, take the germ out
Out of the limelight, taint with discredit and doubt
Weigh the burden down with the system's anvil
Keep his windless voice at bay
Bury him inside the institutional landfill

Our flamed cross will heighten to heaven
If we burn the angels down here
Scatter the oiled rags kissed by kerosene
Over their clipped wings
This memo is an order, is that clear

Truth is purloined perception
Spiced with politics and time to serve the cause
Truth is a stolen cracked heirloom
An arbitrary archive, pilfered memorabilia
Truth is history hiding its flaws

You create truth before truth recreates you
Stifling, where you stand
A round of artillery
A round of applause
For the witness

Scorpio

The Scorpio is anomaly of God
An orphaned child before he is born
Buried beneath the sand, unwanted contraband
Neither animal nor insect in the living creature wars

The Scorpio so feared upon seared Earth
The heavens placed a constellation for him in the sky
Orion falls at the Scorpio's beckoned call
The Scorpio pursues the best of hunters to their demise

Oh, Scorpio, sweet Lothario
Blessed with Ophelia's drowning eyes
Nocturnal sign, vengeance is thine
A curved organ stinger with armored thighs

The Scorpio is the moon's assassin
Though his conquest conjures not a smile
A bandit boy, seductive, without joy
A shameless, melancholy child

The Scorpio, nature's reclusive Garbo
Your entourage cries out for you
The rival of the dove, believing not in love
A disciple to the manipulation that love can do

The Scorpio was a woman born of the water
Outcast from the Rivers of Babylon
Ostracized as society's sore, unholy whore
She survives long after the Biblical days have gone

Like Joan of Arc, the Scorpio knows to pose
In a young man's battle clothes to endure the sun's jealous fire
A lady in disguise with a purpose to paralyze
Any man whom she desires

The Scorpio, fallen victor to the final scenario
The courtship dance is but one web she weaves
Daylight spent beneath desert gold dust,
Brewing her poisoned lust—to wound you as she leaves

Artistic Jester

Mold me, please compose me
Play it as it feels
Or draw the lines, laced with roses and wine
My artistic jester

The palette is his survival
Lyrical sheets reveal an empty song
A mandolin strums the story
Of a love orchestrated so wrong

The heart beats double-four time
A majestic melody
The chorus joins in with laughter
Why is the joke always on me

My artistic jester, paintless memory
Evening greenness, then morning blues
A dead-end resolution
Whichever vignette I choose

My soul drags across the canvass
His overtures crescendo, then dissolve
He hums the fabled riddles
The ones I cannot solve

Ladies swoon with each metered rhythm
Sugar-spun sounds of carnival air
A Mr. Hyde, a Dr. Jekyll
Fair dancers best beware

Oh, the false gestures of the jester
The surreal sadly so real
The harmonious lyre of the liar
His strings unveil my shield

His dark determination is a bright sun shining
My emotional defenses begin to peel
My eyes are running water
Stained along his color wheel

Outdoors Wanting In

A warped woman walks the balanced streets of our town
On a confused path of misdirection
Her thoughts are full of twists and crooked turns
As she talks to shadows of doubt
She sews an imaginary wedding gown
And plans the marital ceremony to perfection
Then those schizophrenic voices remind her
Of what she must forever live without

She sees those loving couples walking hand in hand
Her mind of anguish stops to linger
At those golden nuptial bands
Wrapped around their hearts but not her finger
Another sanctuary of opportunity turns her away
She feels shut out again
Everybody puts the puppy in her proper place
Outdoors wanting in

Oh, how we love to judge the presumed insane
To make our trivial lives seem better
Whenever we grow weary of the contemplation
We simply lock them away
She kept waiting for the ointment of acceptance
To heal the brand of her scarlet letter
No balm of benevolence from her family
Ever anointed her pain

So tonight she lies around
A convenient state asylum
Her least restrictive room is dark and without sound
Though inside her mind is a raging siren
The red lights are blaring down the beat
As her walls of hope cave in
Oh, what a desperate and relentless place
Outdoors wanting in

Outdoors wanting in

Outdoors Wanting In

So pour me another cup of your coffee, please
On this Sunday afternoon, so light and lazy
Let's shake another nut from the family tree
To exhibit inside a bell jar labeled: ETERNALLY CRAZY
Well, it's a pity and shame…
As we stab our own flesh-and-blood in the backs
When we refuse to point to ourselves in blame
While we dig trenches into those vulnerable cracks

Well, you're such privileged husbands and wives
To know what nuclear normalcy is all about
Living your little hypocritical lives
Indoors wanting out

Room Service for One

Surely, you remember our honeymoon hotel
With pink magnolias growing in the foyer
Beneath a portrait of Atlanta burning down like Hell
The Kennedys and the Carters slept here—and you and I as well
At least, those are the anecdotes these four-starred walls love to tell

A cold, hard pain comes pouring down
The cream curtains in lobby drape my memory like your wedding gown
The presence of your absence chills me to the kneeling bone
Oh, baby, loneliness won't quit leaving me alone

No message at the front desk, no answer on your phone
Nothing but an awful lot of nothing for me to do here on my own
I pick up the receiver just to listen to the tone
You'd think I'd have the common sense to keep myself at home

Some love dies with dignity
It slips out like satin in high fashion, elegantly
Some love is like a nylon run that keeps tearing on
Oh, baby, loneliness won't quit leave me alone

The same old suite for lovers, thirteen stories up
The same tea service for two
I pretend to pour a passionate cup
And the same old anxious bellboy, eager to assist me for a buck
I think I'll order room service for one, then beat the furniture up

I flick the TV switch, just for the company of sound
Wheel of Fortune is on the screen, but *U* and *I* are no longer vowels
The presence of your absence is the prime-time feature show
Oh, baby, loneliness won't keep leaving me alone

The AA Train

Watching the mirage of neon beer signs
Dotted alongside this worn-down track
Dreaming of my last shot of moonshine
As the rusty rails beneath my bones crack
And the sobering reality is
The morning after a solo six-pack

I'm riding the AA Train
Over the remaining miles yet to recover
A hangover in a hurry to fade
I'm taking it one step to God knows where
Afraid the truth might be there
To expose me quivering inside this anonymous train

Crossing the burned bridges
Over the support beams my outrages once weakened and wrecked
Closing the final pages
To the horror story my testimony left
The monkey is still on my back shoulders
With both hands clenched around my neck

I'm riding the AA Train
Over the remaining miles yet to recover
A hangover in a hurry to fade
I'm taking it one step to God knows where
Afraid the truth might be there
To point at me, powerless, shaking inside this AA Train

Away, away
Down the lone road
A locomotive pass to an empty glass
A destiny alone

from

Prized Ponies

2000

A Horse of a Different Color

I came across a horse of a different color
A hoof of another hue
I took him by the bridle to become my groom

I met a strapped back covered in black
A steed mounted for the next attack
A galloping grenade—we pulled the forbidden pin—

BOOM   BOOM   BOOM

Oh, before my eyes I could see
A carousel of outcasts revolving me
The argyled, the damasked

A color & style for every taste & task
A trotting tapestry stitching the civil wounds
The needling past had torn thread-thin

Beyond hill, mound, dell, & glade
An escapade in every tolerant shade
A prismatic parade high-stepping to a coming home

I came across a horse of a different color
The sight raised me above the projected blue
I took him by the bridle to become my groom

Prized Ponies

Blue ribbons and badges
Sewn on a sash
Throw youth confetti
Ignore the trash
Prize your young ponies
With all that fine stuff
The real world strips away
Those decorated delusions
In time well enough

Flow of Thought

I sink or sail along the current, Perception
Mystic brew, clear blue, color of the sea
Filling my mind-matter with the hope of liquidity
Downwind of absolute lucidity
The promise of a great river passing
Through the backyard of my foreground
So roll, roll on, Perception
Spill your invisible wine
Pour the overflow into my thirsting eyes anew
And bathe in the cleansing of your freshest waters
Your stream of consciousness whirling into my waking conscience

The Twenty-Five Cent Horse

Place your quarter bits on the quarter horse
Watch him run about the two-bit town
Dangle carats before him when the stakes are high
Kick his fallen flank when he is down

Wager your silver on QuickSilver
When his shimmer fades, turn on him like a dime
The neigh-sayers shoot horses, don't they?
When those manes of magic pass their prime

Cavalcade

Horses on parade
A fine line of thoroughbreds

Promenade
Like sure-footed gods
Greatness gallops in your heads

One in a million
To the vaulted pavilion
Claim the prize in the crowd you desire

Onward, cavalcade
Toward emerald pastures of shade
Oats of gold await when you retire

Bluegrass

Above bluegrass fields
The projectile of a pigskin brings the autumn on
Last summer's color-faded clothes priced and strung
Along jaded bluegrass lawns
The fall equinox presents its annual divide
As sun and moon quietly collide

Blades of bluegrass against my homesick heel
Blades of bluegrass against my homesick heel
A brush with boyhood I fight not to feel
Blades of bluegrass against my homesick heel

Was it Simon or Garfunkel who wrote *My Little Town*
That duet of brilliant boys should lay their pens of pathos down
I strive in vain to listen with nonchalance
I strive in vain to become a man of renaissance

The bluegrass hedges its nostalgic greenery
My mind becomes ether diffusing into the porous scenery
A mental high of anguish caused by a domain displaced
Losing one's mind is another phrase for losing one's place

These intake eyes invent alternative imagery
The bluegrass raked, bundled, and tied
A package refused upon delivery
Still, the song of bluegrass serenades me until death
As bluegrass music pipes into my last breath

French Lick

You came home from the Sorbonne
        with a new kiss on your tongue.
The thesis on Renoir, you claimed,
        had to be redone.
I could have sworn the paper
        was at the cut-and-paste stage.
Or perhaps it is we
        who are at the cut-and-paste stage.

Impressions rise with suspicion
        as I lie down with you.
I recall the painter's proclivity
        for female French nudes.
As you flicker then fold
        against the pink walls of my cheeks,
I am aware of the slight changes
        to your mouth's old theme.

And so this is a sad love song
        for us upon your return.
Your silent lips tell me of a secret in Paris
        waiting your call.
We lapse into revision
        as your sentiments make their debut
On American soil,
        French kisses submitted for suspicion's review.

Whippers & Trainers

Know the difference, my lads,
        between whippers & trainers
Those who prompt you along
        those you push you aside
Those who knead you carefully,
        those who need you incidentally
Those who preach in your face
        those who teach beneath the surface

Note the difference, my lasses,
        between whippers & trainers
Those who mold your mind
        those who scold your behind
Those who won't let you lay waste,
        those who want to lay you for a taste
Those insensitive to your yearnings
        those sensitive to life's turnings

Know the difference, sons and daughters,
        between whippers & trainers
Those who help you hit your stride
        those along for the ride
Those who see your potential
        those who require your credentials
Those who circle when you are lame,
        those who go full-circle in this game

Cantina Sestina

Each weekday at five, I head for The Cantina.
Benito Martinez is the bartender.
My drink of preference, of course, a cool margarita.
I mind my manners and never get drunk.
My favorite thing is nibbling on the glass.
Someone usually presses to play the joint's jukebox.

It is 5: 18: nothing is on the jukebox
as I stroll into my favorite cantina.
A guy shouts, *Hey, buddy, look out for the glass!*
I look toward the bar, but see no bartender—
just Jeb Meyer on a stool; we call him The Drunk.
The love of his life is a good margarita.

Jeb tells me to play *Margarita-*
ville. It is D-16 on the jukebox.
(Now, there's a surprise request from such a drunk.)
A neon light comes on beaming The Cantina.
Suddenly, I see the once absent bartender.
He's mumbling expletives about the broken glass.

To save a few bucks, I bring my refill glass.
and order a Grand Primo Margarita.
Don't hold back on the Cuevo, my loyal bartender.
The Jimmy Buffet tune seeps from the jukebox.
I see the shattered pieces on the cantina
floor. Jeb probably did it—who else but a drunk.

It is now 6:19, and I have drunk
a few Primos from my discounted glass.
The evening crowd spills into The Cantina—
too late to get a buck off a margarita.
The Happy Hour light haplessly dims above the jukebox.
A couple complains to the stone bartender.

Cantina Sestina

Cantina Sestina

Don't whine to me; I'm just the bartender.
Benito retorts as his temper becomes drunk
with anger. He pounds the innocent jukebox.
It's been a long day—what with the broken glass.
I pity him as I sip my sixth margarita.
The neon now dyslexically blurring the words *The Cantina*.

Ah—my sweet cantina, my sweeter margarita!
Benito sweeps the glass behind the jukebox.
Don't look at me, bartender, I'm not the drunk.

Breaker

To pasture or to glue
As if the choice were up to you
A stallion to stud
Slip out of your genes
Share some blood

Night mare or evening sire
Where do you roam when you retire

Mama's little stable boy
Late to the gate, the last to start
To break from the field
You must break some hearts

from

Tender Revolutions

2002

Kitchen Sink

I wake
& dress in raiments
of *Winter Trees*.

At last,
Morning Song
lip-synchs
a dirge ironic.

The oven's door,
Daddy's visage.
It will do.
It will do.

The pipe,
his tongue.
The gas gives him
b r e a t h.

I inhale.
He slips on
my head,
this old black shoe.

        —after the death of Sylvia Plath,
         February 1963

Nuclear Family War

My family is still alive, damn it
The militant positioned to survive another era
Male progeny marching about in Oshkosh B'gosh
The building of soldiers
One Tinker Toy at a time

Tomorrow's women in grandmother's bathroom
Discovering the joys of Lilt
Lathering and rinsing the angels
Out of their cirrus-cloud hair
Tiny mouths talking about the boys overseas
On the other side of the bathtub

Father is an oxygen tank
Gas in, gassed out
An army of one too mulish to follow his own orders
The general is still breathing
This POW checked while on holiday
I wonder, *Who will cut the cord on his accord?*

Mother surveys the remains like a reconnaissance pilot
She swoons about her peremptory rounds
Spot landing to dress unhealable wounds
Her countenance shows regret but no surrender
All the dead have survived, she reports to herself in her sleep
Too bad, though, about the living

Chlamydia

This is my daughter, Chlamydia
Akin to Gonorrhea
Street angel to Syphilis
I bear her every nine lovers or so
Bacterial swaddle in my urethra
A gift from one of three or four Magi
Painful pregnancy
Abortion via antibiotics, shotgun spreading
In my endless spin of promiscuity
She is born unborn again

The child keeps me under wraps
As I slide into the chill of the stirrups
My cervix offering itself to circumspect science
Primping pamphlets on my barren plateau,
The doctor slaps my disease
One mommy
A diary of daddies
I leave her a test-tube orphan at the free clinic
This is my daughter, Chlamydia
Shake hands with the disposables, dear
Wear your pink gloves

Halfway Home

Home Semi-Sweet Home

I step in; I step out
The arc-apex of middle-space is halfway home
I am measured by the distance covered
Front leg first & heel to toe

I move in; I move out
The wheeling cargo is halfway home
I choose the path of most resistance
The miles gone are miles to go

I am in &I am out
This passing fancy is halfway home
I am treaded by the vehicle of trend
Driven by those paving the road

I reach in; I reach out
Free hand in the kitchen jar; I'm halfway home
I take only what occupied time allows me
Clearing the shelf-gardens honest digs have grown

I walk in to first, then head out for third
Second base is halfway home
I want more than kisses from this diamond mound
A virgin-jewel thief on the prowl & probe

I breathe in; I breathe out
One last exhale; I'm halfway home
I have lived to be the death of me
Tripping over light, I fall on stone

The Bell Curve

At the academy,
my daughter sits and broods upon a bell.
Her mind responds, salivates
to the Pavlovian rings.
The tintinnabulations take their diurnal toll.
Her aspirations and aptitude slide
along invisible convexes.
A lean to the right, advanced placement;
a lean to the left, remedial disgrace.

Her playmates become cohorts
bedecked with spectacles, laptops, and a plan.
Our Campanulate sauces homebaked essays.
Salt with assertion, cinnamon with support.
To bed with no dessert
if she inks and plumes a non sequitur
her stepmother and I fail to understand.

I hire her a tutor
to teeter her toward college,
away from the minimum wage.
Perhaps Barron, Kaplan, or PR
will assist us to raise the verbal fields
we are unable to yield at home.

Or perchance all our Angelus needs
to shift to a more auspicious distribution,
a lesson learned in time
when a girl grows curves of her own.

The Respired

Breathing lessons have expired, sound the knell.
Death enters the classroom and tweaks your nose.
In time, you lose the scent but not the smell.

The lungs are last to quit and push to swell.
The air that you breathe at semester's close.
Breathing lessons have expired, sound the knell.

Oxygen gone, students exit pell-mell.
Their huddled bouquet reeks the tone of sorrow.
In time, you lose the scent but not the smell.

So why respire when the throat's afire? Hell,
You'll never learn what the Instructor knows.
Breathing lessons have expired sound the knell.

The aroma of darkness absorbs cells.
You've earned the course credit, now pay off the loan.
In time, you lose the scent but not the smell.

We sniff what the metaphysical sells,
Then suffocate underneath trivial stones.
Breathing lessons have expired, sound the knell.
In time, you lose the scent but not the smell.

Apria

Apria should be the name
of a Greek goddess
whose pulchritude lives by a brook,
not the calling card
of an oxygen-delivery company
that leaves a family breathless
when the lungs are unable
to blacken any deeper,
when the deductible has been met;
but assurance pays no more.

Enter, Apria,
for my father has died.
Grace your loveliness
over this house of mourning-pearl interim.
Extend your winged appendages
to collect the tubes, tanks, and belts—
this hospital bed on loan.
Abscond this hardware, my dad's second skin
from the weathered eyes
of our overcast home.

Then away with you, Apria.
Ascend to your waters
glistening with fresh stone light,
resplendent like a prairie star;
for the strike has darkened
to last smoke on this swollen ground,
where because he has been,
we simply are.

Sadness Is a Place

We learn it as an abstract noun
Intangible to the pupil's optic optimism
Below see-level
An *–ity,* an *–ism,* a *–tude*
A vapor reduced to tears

But Sadness is a place
I have made correspondence of despondence
With its town-and-country face
A miasmic city-state of sorrow
Floating through a deaf sound

Its great, gray smokestacks
Emit monoxide, anti-smells
Noxious, noisome
To tickle the passengers gas-piping in the garage
Too melancholy to complain or cry

Yes, Sadness is a place
You must slow down
To keep up pace
A tourist distraction
Visited by those unafraid of water
With tickets to sigh

ackity-ack-ack

only if
you leave me
will I ever
get you back

nourish, sustain
      sustain, attack

it takes a child
to raze a village
it takes a village
to raise the collapsed

nourish, sustain
      sustain, attack

the camel breaks
from press of water
the arid straw
mends his back

nourish, sustain
      sustain, attack

this game of chess
quotidian Technicolor
black takes white
white takes black

nourish, sustain
      sustain, attack

how   far
from this house of local color
until your pail becomes a bucket,
my brown bag pales into a sack

nourish, sustain
      sustain, attack

                —for CC

The Scheming

I think to scheme and take my scheming slow.
Sleep cannot disturb this perpetual mind
casting players for upcoming shows.

The meditation, a most loathsome ode.
Syrup from my cerebrum salts your eyes.
I think to scheme and take my scheming slow.

You cannot break from this pernicious hold,
demure my lure, despair your prize. My line
casting duped players for upcoming shows.

Your career is at a standstill, a new high-low.
I offer my card; solicit my sins anytime.
I think to scheme and take my scheming slow.

I study your dreams and know what you know.
Your take direction stage left and receive what's condign
as my right brain casts players for upcoming shows.

An offer downstage, you upstage me and go.
The exit is an impasse. Someone should fix that sign.
I think to scheme and take my scheming slow,
casting the players for the late show.

from

Epiphany

2004

___Prologue___

This is time travel of ancient ways,
disciple nights, twelve-star gaze,
the desert step,
walk of three winds,
their prayer, fourth air
sung breath of hymn;
be there beasts, be they wise,
beneath light of fruited sky;
this is Eden, after Eve
He is wrapped and present—believe, believe

January
First Day of Epiphany

A star rings in the East,
brightest toast, confetti sky.
Diapered in snow, Earth a newborn,
balloon-blue.
We three go forth.
Gaspar,
Melchior,
Balthazaar pray…
He isn't king for a day.

February
Second Day of Epiphany

Like a mother in the womb of memory—
herself being born—
we hear a heartbeat.
It rejects the arrow, dismisses myth,
saved by seal of sweet Mary's kiss.

March
Third Day of Epiphany

The wind of a lamb's shake
begins our charmed day.
Shepherds greet us,
descendants of Abraham's ken.
The meekest approaches, prophesizes:
Christ is the lamb who'll be shepherd to all men.

April
Fourth Day of Epiphany

An angel appears,
offers a lily,
places petal on palm.
The sky becomes a dark rose.
We wise are fools, Magi silly.
Tombs taunt princely feet.
Rise, thorn and stone.

May
Fifth Day of Epiphany

Iris hour, open-hand flower,
permits, allows.
We basket earth's gifts—
gold, myrrh, frankincense.
We priests, we astronomers, we believe.
We'll see our king—
as the fruitless Negev
bears faith in spring.

June
Sixth Day of Epiphany

Lady Inquisition summers on evanescent wings—
bugs, stings.
Were we at the manger first night?
Did twelve moons morn?
Perhaps a year hatched—
To Joseph's garden home to jar Herod's swarm!

July
Seventh Day of Epiphany

No fires work the East.
No firmament-fuse cracks the West.
All Israel stilled—
the world, willing, dowses its breath.
Our humbled triumvirate resting, Lord, too—
in honor
in image of you.

August
Eighth Day of Epiphany

We come to Dead Sea,
denied rebirth, drink.
Desiccant stars long, thirst.
A dromedary sips, throat to salt, dirt.
Heat hushes voice-air.
Low body, water, on its knees
in perpetual prayer.

September
Ninth Day of Epiphany

We, too, pupils schooled—
sky, sapphire board—
Star of Bethlehem master, ruler.
Reckoned by discipline,
we pass infinity,
Earth's shortest breath test.
Question in the East.
Answer in the West.

October
Tenth Day of Epiphany

Somewhere, someone inters Immaculate Seed—
It is behind us now;
It is irreversible future.
Gabriel's year to harvest,
glebes of shepherds.
When were we not ripe, God?
Blessed for your picking?

November
Eleventh Day of Epiphany

Famined, faint,
we know not pilgrimage's end.
Dry-mouthed,
we taste the Old Testament,
seasoned exodus.
We step, still, in wonder
of giving leaves.
Lord, we are portions feasting for thee.

December
Twelfth Day of Epiphany

To believe in us now is to tempt theory.
Fit for nativity—
matters us not.
Christ born, here—
Savior, Redeemer.
We, His servants.
We are not gifted.
We are in love.

from

99 Voices, 99 Lives:

County Poems of Iowa

2006

Plow in Oak, Oak in Plow
An Audubon County Poem

Breaking up our team, man and beam, like soil,
        he releases my handle of rustic duty.

In the custody of limbs,
        I pardon him, my farmer, to serve passing troop's call of Civility.

His button-hand soars
        to dress Union shirt sowing freedom's path

to bring glory
        north and home, from brother's bloodied grass.

Exira's winters rust harsh;
        I drift into inanimate life—

and still—I wait and weave the seasons—
        like a long-suffering wife.

My blade roots deep though the trunk's core;
        Come spring, tree cuts a new crown of leaves.

Longing in place, longing in place—
        we suffer from the same disease.

plow in oak—
        oak in plow—

symbiotic shades of grace,
        plod and shroud—

Old Wood, take my last shine, bury me.
        My edge rests its dreams, less and less, I see—

a world of care, a world of peace—chance—
my farmer home to handle me.

Portrait of Chief Black Hawk
A Black Hawk County Poem

I am sitting for my portrait,
Unorganized territory, the frame.
I won't look white flash in its thunder,
but gaze ever eastward, toward Lost Mississippi,
home waters, I one day will reclaim.
My cheeks are primed in oils.
My sorrows stroked in rain.

The brush is still before the war.

Picture it, or paint.

Where are the Sioux and Winnebago?
If Iowa brothers were posed for mockery,
my model cry would die to save their names.
I know return to Illinois will lead to purchase,
but idle squat will do the same.
Sauk tongue is spitting image—extinction, I distaste.
I am sitting for my portrait,
the masterpiece fitting for signature shame.

Glow Depot
A Boone County Poem

Wet, hoarse, from completion of chores,
she lends me her wind, instinct,
warning of words.
Scant light has never shone lesser doubt.

Witness of storm, trestle torn,
she is Mercury the messenger
who must deliver quick speak
of unspeakable account.

I, her sidewick, hang in furious night.

Calmed by her courage,
I kindle what I can.
We cross what carriage remains.
My scout crawls on high ties- - -three-feet apart.
A struck tree of rolling roots barrels our way,
then falls beneath her knees and my flame.

At last, the spoils of Des Moines River behind us,
I clear fire-eating throat,
but not these wicked rains.

She gathers drenched skirts at what must be called shore.
We head for Moingona Depot, near midnight,
with nothing but Impossibility to mount.

Oncoming passenger train, soon, smokes to a stand-steel.

Haloed by darkness, in heroine's hand,
candle of rescue, wick of siege—
I am Kate Shelley's dowsed lantern,
alive, through a child's burning eyes,
saving lives, when urgent frame exclaims,
Four crew men are down, and Honey Creek Bridge is out!

Won't You Marry Me, Hill?
Little Brown Church, Nashua
A Chickasaw County Poem

The only guest
at her bridal shower is God.
She tells him,
For my gift,
let your rains paint me blessedly white.
Her walls have studied
the anatomy of the wedding gown
to each detail, delight.
She knows the custodian's lights-out abandon
escorts out the last of congregate Sunday afternoons—
leaving her to catch lone bouquet-ray,
Sabbath's dying light.

Lady Sanctuary registers at all Nashua newsstands
an eight-piece setting of *now,*
a centerpiece of *soon.*
Wildwood dale, be the pastor;
Borrow, the groom.
Blue bells, comes the bride
drawn at the waist
by the weight of cathedral tombs.

Her train is a lawn of pressed lilies –
patience has grown
with the witness of water
and shade's stoic trill.
Sachets of scented rice
perched like lovebirds
on each window sill.

The Little Brown Church in the Vale
prepares to marry—
                                      but she never will.

Among the Brome of Autumn
A Decatur County Poem

Among the brome of autumn, I down my wintry home,
Beak to spur, my trench unstirred, a few hours from first snow.

A cocked gun swells, sport of smell,
I've heard declare before.
Hunter routes German pointer,
A theater for war.

Old World birds fill scenery.
Endangered, my allies,
Speak to me, so quietly,
Of death-stalk in the sky.

The grouse is a bit mottled,
But he cannot complain.
Bobwhite on look-out's tell-wire
Warns of All Saints' shell-rain.

Gestapo spots his rooster.
My brood stills as if unborn.
I alight from grace and fright
Above the standing corn.

The gauge is at the ready.
Season tolls to doom's boom-sound.
I fall to earth, gauge my worth,
Oh, captor, of high ground.

Hunter, leave me dignity.
Remove not my red mask.
Waste not my feral being.
This is all that I ask.

Cold marksman's blade, resting shade,
Flense my warm breast apart.
Give to me clean dignity.
I, pheasant, give my heart.

Among the Brome of Autumn

Among the Brome of Autumn

The partridge sings to free me,
But I am more than free.
Celebrate on caroled plate.
I wing to fruited tree.

Among the brome of autumn, I down my wintry home,
Beak to spur, my trench unstirred, a few hours from first snow.

Hobo Convenience Store
A Hancock County Poem

A boxcar of us fits like a six-pack—
Refrigerated, inseparable souls.
We bed newspapers, brown bags, trash plastic.
Stories we tell glaze a few donut holes.

Life's a fountain of unlimited refills.
So's we've been dispensed like cubed and crushed ice.
You won't spot up hurtin' back in work's break room.
That's just wiper-fluid gushin' down our free-loadin' eyes.

Hot Dog! Britt is a breath mint, come August.
The proof's in the hooch we call Railsplittin' Pop.
Our hard swallows return to cappuccino—
When sad tracks depot near Sunday blue laws.

We come and go just like you gourmet folks…
Drizzlin' quick milk and gone-by gas on us.

Amity of the Amanas
An Iowa County Poem

An historian told me Amity is the Sweetheart of the Colonies,
But I believe she remains its Truest Soul.
Benevolent Miss founds at no legal residency.
Among concord locals is but one of possible homes.
Look for Amity's gather at tables, friendly bread.
Seek her fellowship in cellars of Welcome's wine.
She is faithful greeting at Every Street.
Good News, facing East, with gravestones, at the Lord's first shine.

Like all things, ambitious and abstract—
Amity nears Anger's domain, but there her business will not settle.
Where has Fraulein Lily gone? Gaze Iowa's Seven Wonders, inspired tourist,
Search homestead, ox-field, Rise and West, gaze both High and Middle.
Amity folds when peace is in need, of this attraction be most aware—
Constant she lives—where a heart forgives between two hands in prayer.

The Smolder of Old Stone
A Johnson County Poem

Pick a plum of respite.
Pick a plum of repose.
The territory rests its case.
A state awaits Plum Grove.

Iowa City, IA, November 20, 2001—

The University like a map is not the territory
you once blazed with fiery legislation,
the brim of a dream,
fervid promises of honest work.

This evening, abandon is a capital crime.
Fueling the news—*The Burning of Old Capitol*—
a grassfire sweeping across the Pentacrest and prairie,
from the flame of tenured tongues,
over autumn's lectern, to erudite neophytes,
who break before Thanksgiving break,
to contemplate the smoldering of Old Stone.

It is the season of rescue;
we are all armed with water.
As your beheaded dome plunders,
Sister Heritage, this hour, loses a tip
of her golden touch.

The symbolism of a state dissipates.
Our assignment for tomorrow, symbiology,
but who has time to study it much?

Children of a Lesser Sod
A Lyon County Poem

Is this the last stop of the Orphan Train, God—
Northwest Passage out of Iowa, the final depot?

Has the state run out of heart and Heartland—
Is there nowhere else to go?

We've heard Dakota winds are wild—
Terror rides mightily through vengeful Sioux.

Can you please keep us here, Lord?
Anything Governor Cummins can do?

Are there really lions in this county?
That wouldn't be so bad,

We'd make the finest cubs—
at least, we'd have moms and dads.

A den at Inwood roars with us most excellent.
We bet Rock Rapids has a proud Mane Street—what could it hurt?

To us children of a lesser sod, us gutter swipes,
we brush-offs bound for a clean sweep of rejection's dirt.

And we've come so far, Father,
like a Nor'easter blowing in from New York.

We know tiny tongues should not car-by-car complain
on westbound train when the conductor is our Lord.

But we've taken a liking to Iowa—place us out
to the squats who gave us scarves and fruit.

If it's good enough for corn,
why can't we, new family tree, take acre and root?

We'll say our prayers on the hour,
read the *Children's Bible,* stop sucking nervous thumbs.

This our pledge, God, as we stand on this choose-me caboose,
throwing to our lost parents, a last station of crumbs.

Loess Hills
A Monona County Poem

Perhaps this is where ice comes of beauty and age.
Perchance this is where a border calls bluff, and both stoop to pray.
Or, maybe, Paul Bunyan fell from a high plain—
Yes, maybe, these catsteps prowl his grave.

Perhaps China has a dark side to its Great Wall.
Perchance this is where moles raise the roof for an annual ball.
Or, maybe, this is where the sculptors to the gods
Gather their magical clay.

The Loess Hills are everything
That old, crumbly schoolbook said they would be.
Loess Hills make silk and dirt
The same.

Ah, but these moon-cat hills,
Mount Lovelies, are not some to call
My Antonia's return to me.

You've crossed the Mighty Mo'. Haven't you, love?
You're hanging up a homestead with Nebraska's favorite son.
Silt and guilt cannot summon you to come back to me, come.

I was not Jill's chosen.
Just a tumble-tantrum Jack

                falling down—

eroding

eroding

erosion....

Floppy Dish
A Polk County Poem

Unhushable puppy, that Floppy,
Big-mouthed beagle in a box,
Pound puppet, born from balsa wood,
And one lovingly knit red sweater—
In 1957, his master, Duane Ellett unleashed him on WHO-Channel 13,
The mutt was a natural, amidst those makeshift sets—
You never saw him blink—
By the 1960s, Floppy was a staple,
An after-school snack at 3:30, best babysitter to the bone,
You could count on him, 1 to 10, more than your teacher or friends—
Sick days were not in his contract,
And his sitting fees, reasonably free—
He has his occasional co-star,
Uncle Taffy, Standeen, Scary Mary,
The Inspector, Matilda the Bookworm,
And a few rivals, up north in Ames,
Betty Lou Varnum's *Magic Window*
With Katrina Crocodile and Gregory Lion;
But he never was one to growl about the ratings—Beep his nose—
He thought the Nielsen's was a show on prime time—
Never angered, only a child's kiss made our brown best-boy blush—
And Channel 8's Mary Brubaker, girlfriend, now you know,
Upon you Floppy dished a Capital Crush—
Unlike other legends of the screen—
Carson, Wayne, Russell, Reed—
Floppy didn't take his talent one paw out of the state,
And like a certain cat to his favorite flakes,
Iowans young and old thought Duane and pal were more than ok,
In fact, it was the public, we humans, who barked, picketed
When executives pulled his 30 minutes
And millions of moppets' jokes off the air—
Outside beleaguered station in downtown Des Moines,
Mothers in enraged curlers, babes in Floppy T's and underwear—
Thanks to Floppy, America had the biggest pencil in the world—
And cars weren't just cars, those rods rode hot—
His giggles were cold milk and warm cookies on a mundane afternoon,
Thanks, Mom, and quality television, that really hit the spot—
Floppy was Prince and Fido; but, mostly, Floppy was King—
Duane Ellett had not something, but someone extraordinary up his sleeve,
And Floppy, the Pinocchio puppy, had central Iowa on a string.

Letter from United Flight 232
A Woodbury County Poem

July 19, 1989

Dear Advice Columnists:

Question:

All three hydraulic systems down,
a stormy witch spells with her broom.

Surrender, steering! So long, elevation!
All on board destined to die!

I am most able captain.
I am least able passenger. What do we do?

Signed,
Two of Sioux City Doomed.

Answer:

Do not forget.
Faith is its own etiquette.

First, pray for flat land—God's abundant lay in Iowa,
not even the bluffs roaming the river can deny.

Then, think as long as you can—
This aircraft is spirit.

You keep it as long as you can—
in His clearest blue sky.

from

On Holiday

2007

Cardinal Rules

The cardinal is the Christmas bird.

He takes birth-blood to wing—

To color a world on holiday—

Upon dusted boughs of evergreen.

Airing Christmas Laundry

The myth will rinse; when it cleans, the lint knows
Old stories from Santa won't wash the air
And, still, kids cling, stubborn as static snow

Parents basket the blunders, quick to tow
The wet disappointment, the bleaching stares
The myth will rinse; when it cleans, the lint knows

Hampered by betrayal, children red-glow
A sort-and-separate eye to fading fare
And, still, kids cling, stubborn as static snow

Hung out to dry from the cold-water soak
A fluff, a fold—cycle, leaves children bare
The myth will rinse; when it cleans, the lint knows

Folks forgiven for dirty linen, though
Some stains remain, tumbling, to stiff despair
And, still, kids cling, stubborn as static snow

We begin our spin—kids believe the load
Left on the line, pinned, with fine lies to spare
The myth will rinse; when it cleans, the lint knows
And, still, kids cling, stubborn as static snow

Poor, Pitiful Pearl

Named for a concealed gem,
hardened by desperate times,
in the assembly-line ocean,
she is hooked and lured
by icons of Poverty and Concern
to live the rest of her days
as a peculiar doll on Earth.

An anachronism to those
who have gone toy-fishing,
her tawdry orange hair, irregular face,
more fit the Great Decline of the 30s.
Poor, Pitiful Pearl is out of place
in the aisle and age of first Barbies,
even within the discount bin—ordinary disgrace.

And on her sullied hem,
a scarlet patch, not unlike Hester Prynne,
who can match Pearl's disbelief to the letter,
for it is not little girls, little girls who buy
this would-be-retail reject
too impoverished to wear a costume disguise—
no, not little girls, but grown women
who through their 1950s furs, fat purses remember—

When nothing in the kitchen stewed,
FDR announced entry in World War II,
and not even a stocking or whiskered tree stirred
in their pale houses of bleakest Decembers.

Matchless

After Hans Christian Andersen's THE LITTLE MATCH GIRL

What light. what heat
sticks like friction
in hungry hair—
no match for Despair.

Old Amsterdam—

I stand before the hoary corpse
of the Little Match Girl,
hung holly, sad sulfur.

Breaths of despair,
my wet boots attend
in storybook wonder.

If only I had purchased
a fascicle of her wares,
No.

If only I had been sufficient wind
to avert strike, her father's fury,
No.

If only I were the fire
she could not
put out.

Nivea Campana

Henry Wadsworth Longfellow wrote the poem Christmas Bells,
later to be the lyric, I Heard the Bells on Christmas Day, *on Christmas Day, 1863,*
while nursing his son, Charles, wounded in the Civil War.

He had an ear for war, that Longfellow,
knowing no two forms, like snowflakes, were ever alike—

Holocaust home for the holidays,
cannon flickering o'er candled-kegged windows,

a peal of sable-scarved cardinal
bloodying the yuletide sky.

Gave him the quills. Broke serenade into accursed song.

He had a belfry for lyric, that Longfellow,
a wounded son and nation remembered on every line—

Hollow Christmas Eve, 1863,
Gettysburg and son, Charles, in a sling—doleful snow, doleful snow.

Pale epitaphs bunched, forted,
building old, familiar dirges on high.

Kept the man at home fires, away from the caroling throng.

He had an ear for silver, that Longfellow,
the kind that flanked Christendom, then rang from the chest.

Holy Ghosts scrooging around elsewhere in England,
what rightful apparition could redress this civil wrong?

Predatory bells tolled the passing,
bleak season drifted on hungry tongues—

The first chime was *ding*. The dead ringer was *dong*.

—for Great Great Grandfather James Francis Hindes
Union Soldier, United States Civil War

Elveswhere

The elves don't dance
in me wintering dreams.
Their agile agendas
simply *tee-hee-hee* refuse.

Sprig-like sprites
won't light one ignite
in me reverie hair—
What's yuletide yawner to do?

I've nary a fairy
up me slumbering sleeve—
'Tis true.
'Tis blue.

I wake to slip on
me sorry soles—
Oops!
Two are in me shoes!

The Skate at Scholte Gardens

As the good folks of Pella
simmer down in mid-December,
for a gentle, concord snow—
the bronze statues at Scholte Gardens
rise to life, from iron, despite the tin of record lows.

The gardener boards his trusty bike
to enter the wintry gate
and wonder of chilled flowers.
Grown lady and daughter stowed
behind her quite copper dress,
reborn as human forms,
though keep it quiet,
for it is after-hours.

And the two cast tulips
a boy of brass offers in blooming hands,
they change into a pair of wooden skates.
He slips them on like woolen stockings,
glides about the iced brick lawn—
but not in the usual figure *8s*.

An *S* for snow,
An *S* for Savior,
Then Boy Brinker judges himself a pause—
to catch fresh breath
for the biggest *S* yet—
one for Sinterklaas.

Gardener, Woman, Daughter
gather around such Dutch performance of astound—
a gesture of gratitude to deliver—
there, at the boy's, momentary, flesh feet
a fallen treat—
tulips of bell and silver.

Iceberg Rose, Greenwood Rose Garden, Des Moines

There, among an ocean floral-bed, Book of Dreams,
Tahitian sunsets, and Starry Nights,
You spot the dispassionate beauty—
And your frigate for romance come-hithers
Toward her frigid fragrance.

Flirtatious tip, she reveals, at best
Ten percent of total floral cluster—
But that is enough glacial-gather
To trip your maiden voyage,
Freeze you in your dinner jacket.

Starboard, the prow of your nose brushes her side—
Aromatic collide, flower to your fancy,
Lady breaks a bit—
Just enough to tear olfactory senses of all passengers—
Appreciation, up-turned in First Class—
                                        curiosity in lower ranks.

Her battering bouquet sinks into your hull of memory.

Witness clouds as lifeboats   ported in an odorless sound.
Cold April, like first temptation,
Comes late this season, and so you inhale, and so you drown.

Captain, captive,
Your breath will never reach penance—
                                    —at far side of garden harbor.

Nearer to God, nearer to God—
You cry for a smell,
But it is she of spring's sea
Who is resistant of Arctic water
And the warm blood of men.

Her white habit could save souls—
Or devour them.

Albino Deer, St. Ansgar, Iowa

The Dickens of the Forest,
she may have seen three ghosts
on morning
of her spring birth—
they who scared, whitened, and seized
the color of her frame.

For eight years,
the chalk fawn removed paint
from dark timber lines between Minnesota, Iowa—
she who saw red at humankind's artistry—
keeping notes on her skin,
the tint of alabaster flakes.

Fifteen upstart tails, she present-bore.
They would color-call her mother,
though none of them, none of them
to take her pallor-shade.

Nearly invisible all of her life,
our deer would not quite disappear
like that one cloud of future-wonder
on an, otherwise, blue day.

But those ghosts reappeared,
like the slip of glass in winter—
trio of haunts
to wither her to cold cinders:
pneumonia, kidney failure, and old age.

The Hierarchy of Angels
The Devil is general; angels are specific.

God, being universal, delegates discrete authority,
Establishes functional hierarchy among the strata of angels.

The Trinity,
Obsessed with Triumvirates,
Spawns Three Spheres:

Bearers of God's Thrones, Priests, and Ministers.
Each Sphere wings Three Orders:
*
BEARERS
Gabriel (the brass go-between) and Cherubim (winged singers beneath God's breath)
Dancers of the intellect for the Omniscient Mind

The Seraphim (celestial serpents)
Breathers of heaven's fire, the eternal, not infernal kind

The Thrones (mirrors of the Lord's justice)
Minders of the quake, unshaken by the raptures of being
*
PRIESTS
Dominions (Divine bureaucrats)
Integrators of the spiritual and material, governors of reality

Virtues (beams for dreams)
Keepers of spiritual truths and treasures, God's trove of priceless chattel

Powers (collectors of conscience, drummers of duty)
Mighty mentors to soldiers of Earth's inevitable dirt, battles
*
MINISTERS
Principalities (Weathered ones of our upper ether)
Guardians, good for all groups—cities, nations, all of God's creations

Archangels (Blessing the down four-limbed creatures)
Shepherds to speechless, humankind's ablest teachers

At last, Angels
Lowly angels, bone-specific, still we laud them on high
Each a god on cross guard, until we are permitted to walk the streets of the sky

As on a Wintry Plain

The ghosts won't haunt, still you lift a ride,
take a team of eight by gossamer reins,
colorless journey, save the chestnut sleigh,
through barest of birches, no limbs to hide,
except your sparse bones in their waning lives,
to scarve you or scar you, whatever pain
that will encourage the ghosts to mush again,
their eyes of white wolves running in full stride.

What keeps you, child, on such long, wintry plain—
the blush ahead is not one of summer;
it is last regret, a light in the fog,
to give you false wish, a fool's wonder.
The ghosts break for last bits of prairie grain,
then forward lift toward the face of God.

Bethlehem, Pennsylvania

First and forever born—
A night, a year, an age.
Mother is on maternal leave 'til spring.
Father is a new-hire wage.

And there, child, you lie, transfixed
In Mid-Atlantic manger down.
To the up-East, a star lights off Broadway/
To the West, the steely haunts of Allentown.

Absent beasts quicken to warmer prairie.
Angel of Mercy booked in Hollywood.
Circling around you, kid, hand-me-down Lionel trains,
And your first pair of crocheted workman's boots.

Yes, Aunt Philadelphia is at her Christmas knitting.
She stews upon a skittish stool.
In this evening of hurt—Behold, a shirt—
She twists the collar blue.

Outside, the factories are stacked against you, child,
Like the odds of getting good meat on next noon's plate.
Nightshift snow angels make blades of iron.
Flakes of smoke fall on their haloes of keystone gray.

Three drug dealers have walked the urban desert
To crack the addict's call.
Pop Joe needs a hit of amyl anything.
Ma Mary, a dose of Demarol.

Such steel-clad clarity, narcotic nativity,
Strung out like Auntie's yarn.
Another boy born in discounted basement,
Another baby in the barn.

The Mother of Trees

God refused to fit her in evergreen fir,
so she slips on the ice for winter kills—
haggard branches, egg-empty,
rock-candy coated, gossamer gloved,
nesting nothing but wicked debris.

Bereaved, her hanging glass
crosses the wires, detours the streets.
Chaos and crystal in freeze-frame,
she leans.

Her children long left her,
seeking fleeting careers in bags of leaves.
Her husband, faithless as summer;
nothing, but hard wind, to solicit as lover.

Snow blind from spring,
the mother of trees
heavies as she blows,
bereft in clinging beauty,
foreboding pose.

She crackles like a hidden witch,
bends her broom over the pitch roof,

and breaks the stone house

where a once beloved family

once trusted her roots.

The Snow Geese

the snow geese
precipitate the sky

with   winter
                wings

V-trekked,
beak direct,
any route, but circumspect

a rage of horns resounding
across the one true open road

flurrious flock
insistent that fall yield
the right of way

their down drifts
across the dark lake
of frosted reeds,
& the last departing loon

autumn abandoned,
the gaggle rules,
accumulates in a solstice sky—
their cornet's cry
announces in stentorian tune

He   He
     as   as
        we

comes again
& soon!

I Am a Poor Boy, Too

There is a boy in the desert

Keeping time on animal skins

He is wise among kings and their riches

He worships a babe in the barn

His coat is sparse, but of many blunders

Poverty, neglect, wounds

He is night wind and little lamb

Lowly eye of the sky

There is a boy in the desert

Kicked among gold and myrrh

And when, at last, he turns from the manger

It is he who inherits the earth

Reach me

Ah, for the music they die

Teach me

Or is the counselor I

My rhythms

Silent dusk's only tune

Please, boy,

Touch my full lain moon

There is a call for you, too

Count on me, calmly

With my one need

Beat me

from

Titanic:
A Centenarian Voyage in Verse

2011

Belfast Shipyard

Steel frame is laid; fat contracts signed.
If ticks past six, it's overtime.
We'll work until the foreman does his horning—
A thousand days,
Three-thousand men,
A ship of dreams
From bow to end.

Iron will be rising in the morning.

God bless this girder, beam to beam.
Steer her from harm out on the sea.
Take her Trans-Atlantic to torch's shoring.
We march to make.
Beat the bodhran.
Oh, gather 'round,
Green Irish sons.

Iron will be rising in the morning.

She's inching now to scrape the sky.
Pinch me if there's lovelier eye.
Each rivet is a gift that's worth adoring.
The hull, her soul;
The keel, her spine.
You find her heart,
You'll find mine.

Iron will be rising in the morning.

The *Titanic* Stowaway

The more fanfare, the finer a diversion.
Look at them, greeting and parting,
Clawing at confetti
Like the last clutches of land
All arrogant aboard!

Perfect British weather
For a *bon voyage* orphan.

That 1912 Debauney-Belleville about to load
Requires no driver,
Yet a confidant rider, like me, fits
Beneath its boards,
Below the lowest of the third-class.

I'm the cousin to the uncle of his sister.
That is who I am—
Should anyone ask.

There Were Never Enough Lifeboats

A fact and a matter

Walk into a Southampton street bar.

Try as they might,

Their brandied breaths are unable

To keep concerned conversations

For the loaded passengers

Afloat.

Eastertide, 1912

All things aboard *Titanic* were as fresh
as the last coat of paint, save the lilies.
Potted in aged bronze, or pressed between *Psalms*
the elegant white arches were sacred remains
of Easter, some three mornings past.
Lilies of lace and surrender
lifted and rose in nearly every state room, alcove,
a testament to season, partner in color to porcelain,
each inflorescence blended divinely
with the dishes at the last supper.
Spreading their petals like innocent hands, across tables,
as if to say, *Take this vision, in remembrance of me.*

Oh, let there be white wines, whiter bread.
Let there be light for the grave impasse ahead.
And allow a cross for the water lily
as it trespasses the sea.

But, alas, this ship will know nails.
Horrified hemispheres regale in shaming sermons, the tales,
the loss of each lily as it sinks
in cold communion to the monstrous ministry.

God Himself Could Not Sink This Ship

I prefer to work alone,
the shifting portents of tides and sky,
continuous rhythms of My labors
in a world I plan to leave behind.

You have constructed your cities,
smoked the guns to your industrial races,
claimed your ticketed inventions, yourselves,
without any nod to your God and My graces.

Yet, this is still My arena.
It is My coliseum.
I see your bread and circus has taken to water.
Funnels and fanfare aside, I shall do as I please.

Hubris and Arrogance—
sport such fine chariot horses.
Mid-voyage, I shall storm these chartered reins,
force their steam-snorts down a deviant course.

To crystallize My point,
clarify My good word,
your state-of-the-art bow will bow
in old testament to the primitive iceberg.

Is *Genesis* not sufficient evidence?
The fall of Adam and Eve not enough for your doubtful employ?
What I have created—
I, too, can destroy.

The Iceberg Has a Word

If I am
an ancient
child of the earth,
then you, fresh ship,
in the cycle of things,
bow-to-stern, are certain to be
a spiteful child of mine.
I see you have taken my giving waters,
set sail on some fanciful invention, design.
It is approaching midnight;
and you on your maiden voyage of menace
approach this parental-polar territory of mine.
Come, child. Come, closer.
My—it has been such a long time.
Why the hurry? Why the rush?
Speed of two dozen knots, not a propeller to spare
for a gash or gush?
I am still ice, still your father. Behave or beware.
The night is moonless; no waves are breaking.
And the stars are merely flirting for the true forsaking.
I can ground you with a single unflinching stare,
send you down, down the ocean's winding stair.
Go, there, to your room. The morning papers headstone your tomb.
Like a bruising bully, I will only strike you from below.
Nothing for the social busybodies to detect, nothing to show.
Now, go there, to your room. It's 2 AM, and past your curfew.

Ticket to Survive

If you have a fur,
an animal wrap of any kind,
wear it.
Act feminine and old,
exhale chilling charms
with and beneath your frost breath.
Speak of your grandchildren
awaiting in the Hamptons
and coddle whatever little lambkin
meadows nearest your breast.
Turn and walk elegantly.
Tell the maid, curtsied and cold,
upon return to your parlors,
you'd like some warm tea.
Don't bother tipping the crew.
Your money won't float here.
And despite your icy arrogance,
it is their blind eye owing you apology.

Dress Formal for Casualty

Our tails, tip-stiff, watertight corsets bound.
Lifeboats hang like swing threads, mid-air ferry.
Who will be best dressed in black, buoyant gown?
Jackets worn not for life, but to bury.

Such cruelty to cargo, April caused
Virgin linens to lose lungs in wintry pool.
Fine dishes expired before serve's first course—
Unnerving cello strings, plunged strings of pearl.

Cold chap, do you see white stars line the sky?
Forgive nature's 'berg, not man's numb rudder.
Cast into tombed night, we the ostracized
Banned from breath's sight, climbing on one another.

All we can say of with whom we sink—
In blue garden, like Eve, she, too, was weak.

(Lying to)
Women and Children First

It is not so much an act of chivalry,
or even protocol,
to claim or call
women and children first.

It descends from *Birkenhead* circa mid-1800s,
a borrowed line, White-Star lie,
an expressed euphemism
in wake of true cataclysm, a castaway hearse.

There, they are…
the swinging lifeboats
dangling precariously
to the ragtime music on outer deck.

The rich, indeed, are different.
And they are nothing, if at least, suspect.
You must give them something
lest they nickel-and-dime detect.

The crew speaks of mere practice,
some archaic English code
to test the twenty runt-rockers
in the fiercest night of cold.

It is not one step for man,
but two for woman and scant-year-old
this evening of craterous collapse
a maiden miscue nearly tantatmount
to the virgin-voyage of Jesus

as the greatest ship-scripture ever told.

Fifth Officer Harold Lowe's
Blessing Those Without Boats

After the sea leviathan glinted her last lashes of attack,
After armies of ocean swords buckled and dragged her down to private bleed,
I gathered and tied nearby lifeboats 4, 10, and 12 into a flotilla a mutual support,
Transferring the transfixed more closely together, so lifeboat 14, alone, could be free.

We, the makeshift crew, rowed back among the dead and the feeble crying.
We rowed back into an ash-raking of blue-and-white leaves.
Most poignant were the oars, deft and considerate, not to touch the breathless passing.
It was the most touching moment of my service to the unassailable sea.

Gliding between shoals of subsided souls, who seemed like mannequins
Inside fate's freeze-frame store window, wearing tragedy's cloaks and hats,
It was a kind of reckoning reconnaissance, surveying the long-but-short suffering,
Each dip into the decided dilemma, an offering, an apology—if that.

Inspection became benediction. I believe we rescued three—faith, hope, and charity.
We duped ourselves into the possibility of more boats, other ships to remedy this loss—
That these stiffened existences were just likenesses of those we had met on the decks.
It was too dark to see true evil, so we stroked, we stroked, in course shape of a cross.

Isidor and Ida Straus

It is said *Titanic* can travel up to 24 knots.
We, Isidor and Ida Straus, prefer to travel as one knot.

Those are not lifeboats entering the sea,
but floating devices descending to separate the inseparable.

The iceberg, indeed, is a blue-veined mistress,
splitting up the ship from its tattered passengers—

but she only interlaces our lives, hand-overhand,
to sure harbor, steadfast land.

What travel is this,
to embrace and accept our voyage to the eternal world.

Infernal, icy waters enter the deck as dagger-fountains,
ripping and wrenching all loosely formed ties.

A moment's disaster cannot unbind
these 40 years of Macy's fame, fortune—the feast of family.

Charitable strings of the orchestra
play our song of love and lament.

Had we been poor,
there was never an hour more richly spent.

We are dying together, more tightly, closely
than the clench of any cold could ever entomb–

soul slipping into soul, bodies bent.
Death is dessert, and here, here—lie in wating

two perfect
silver spoons.

Rhymes with Ocean

All of love is motion,

And the only movement here—

The manufactured waves

Of the tragic monolith,

Descending from the vested sacrifices

It required

To trap in its passion, its quest

For the cold ocean bedding.

At last, at rest—

How moving the stillness,

Lovely, this absence of remorse,

As if deep travel, indeed, removes memory

Of the heightened fury

Our aboveboard world will not soon be forgetting.

Wallace Hartley, Leader of the Band

The only tips our band received that night to remember

were from the iceberg itself, cold coins indeed,

shards serving as precursors to the failing of that ship.

Calm, I told myself. Gather the fellow musicians and play

as if the evening were still on the go.

We formed behind the first funnel, by the Grand Staircase.

I called for selections of suites and waltzes by number,

just as the summoning sea called its victims by number.

Light and lambent arrangements strung the hastening foot beats.

The orchestra played on, lifeboat after lifeboat

leaving the vicinity of our sound. Those loading were never to know

which was the last song, *Nearer My God to Thee,* or *Songe d'Automne.*

I bade the gentlemen farewell.

The bridge, interluding verses of life and death, came crashing in.

A captain at sea goes down with his ship.

A leader of the band goes down with his violin.

The Unsinkable Molly Brown

That evening was not the dawn of suffrage.
It was the dawn of suffering.
Being a river girl from Hannibal, Missouri,
The Mark Twain in me knew what to do with an oar.

Stiffer than the bodies spearing the North Atlantic,
Our disbelief inhibited any due course.
Lifeboat No. 6 lay there, transfixed, half-occupied,
A tacit witness of the overture, overboard.

Row! I told the grieving gals. *Row!*
Riding first class had saved my ass.
We had to distance ourselves from the sinking diva
Before our return to survey for survivors.

I quarreled with Quartermaster Hichens,
Like a dress hat full of hornets,
To bring the boat back among the drowning—
After the great ship had cleared.

We women were unable to sable-muffle our ears
To his pessimism and complaints.
He criticized the dead and dying as stiffs—
And, there, the blue-hued should remain.

I never took guff from my husband in Denver.
And I was about to jettison the junk
That steered *Titanic* starboard
When she was better off left head-on with berg.

But he knotted me tongue-tied, out to sea,
Once he, that craven navigator,
Offered to exchange his bullets
For my save-all-souls words.

Broadway billed me *Hello, Molly, the Unsinkable, the Queen of Cork;*
The weight of fame anchored me
Like a steamer full of corpses and coals.
First Lady of the Lifeboat—

Isn't fitting in New York, one day, I die of a stroke?

Jude Descending the Grand Staircase
After X. J. Kennedy's *Nude Descending a Staircase*

Break upon break, a salted flesh
With club of flame and leaded mind,
St. Jude sifts through flotsam down drowning stairs
To congregate prayers for the left-behind.

He spies beneath carved banister
To witness God's will and wash on high rise;
He dips an offering, eternal air
To the nostril-pooled and floating passers-by.

Apostle-Waterfall, he wears
A rare drapery of ocean mosses
To rope the hopeless from frosted sea—
This blessed saint of lost causes.

Titanic **Doll**

Porcelain should make one dispassionate,
a manufactured actress
who does not wet or feel—
removed from the pulse of playtime,
bantam-butterfly blinks goodnight.

I have lost her, the girl.

I know her only by touch.
Never trust a doll's eyes.

How can I call out for her hands?

There are nothing but hands flapping and flinching
like flensed seals.

I do not want a mermaid nurse-mommy.

I am not impressed by this marine arena,
Neptune's playhouse.

I am dressed for story time
and prefer the predictable ending.

I miss her spoiled pout.
What must be current is washing away—
the smile painted between my cheeks.

The sea is a shell.
I can hear home in my ears.

I will require no further changing,

I do not need this ocean
to be soaking in tears.

Trolling for Bluefish

Nearly a week in the wake,
an aftermath of disaster—
a cable ship is summoned
to the sinking grounds,
to survey, bring to dry lot, the dead.

The deceased, for the most part, are there,
coagulated like white blood cells,
still full in their vests
from being served
primitive nature's cold dish.

The cable casts its line,
attached with blessed-baited hooks,
the bereaved collected like a school of bluefish,
fanciful fins, learning, too late,
the harshest of lessons, from the sea's oldest book.

Sanding the Lifeboats

What arrives to sanded shore is shameful, symbolic—
progressive arrogance, cost-cutting indifference,
the inevitable stroke-fall of humankind to nature.

And there,
like thirteen beached disciples of defeat,
lie the remains of *Titanic's* standard lifeboats
in their signature nomenclature.

Hasten, you handymen,
remove the sullied nameplates,
scrub, sand, and abrade
the printed paint of her tainted name.

Then, hoist and stow the boats high,
in a dark warehouse that treads time.
Prevent evidence from leaking
the tidal arrival of liability claims.

The Blue Period
After Picasso's THE TRAGEDY, 1903

A painter worth his ocean salt could rework this landscape,
the raking light, three somber figures with arms folded on blue-sanded beach.
Perhaps more survivors of the shipwreck are in sketches, underneath.
And something about the monochrome sky, here, refuses to reach.
It aches in its witness; it shows the sum nothing of destructions
in a flat rain, the color, its engineer would swear, of watertight pain.
Immobility gains a stroke of momentum in the creation's reduction.

The child is speaking here, as if to whisper, *I was here first.*
It was the sad captain's last order before he vanished, dispersed.
A woman in a blackberry shawl looks into the mop's shoeless feet.
She realizes the boy's prints are just scratching a shattering surface.

And the man here wears bruised garments soaking in death.
He, like the sky, did not reach this shore. His misery did not survive.
Yes, a painter worthy of the region could rework this landscape with one brush of ice.

The Revenant Ship

In the closing folds of April, she arrives,
bearing the hallowed and hypothermic
to a discharged harbor occupied solely by
jetsam confetti and flotsam welcome signs.

For a fortnight, she's held her hull-breath,
passed tragedy's nautical test,
to address a media, a world
that only cares how the redoubtable died.

Scumbled and sacked,
only hanging chandeliers remain intact,
she is pressed to find a pedestal
that will place her back on original design.

For the sleep of her passengers, she embeds all humankind,
then descends back where she belongs, into the cryptic brine.

Dr. Robert Ballard Discovers the Hitherto Famous
September 1, 1985

Like Garbo,
she has gone to great depths
to be alone with the abalone.

There,
in secluded seawater estate
Titanic couches inside her dark parlor.

Time,
her most trusted servant,
like a panicked passenger, at last, deserts her.

She hasn't a soul.
It has been divided,
ripped with the wreckage, scattered among debris, bones.

Still,
the mistress ship feels a presence,
a sense of unwelcome science floods her.

Intrusive, incisive—
blinking submersibles
photograph her privacy like bush-popping paparazzi.

At her anchored age,
it has become abysmally clear:
Deep in the blackest of green, the sea is its own silver screen.

And the silent, sunken propellers were nothing—
but shrieking fans all along,
manic-magnets pulling the public back to her.

A Partial Colossus
After Emma Lazarus' *The New Colossus*

Titanic was to consort with my torch,
bring to me her tiered wealthy, pugnacious poor,
heralded masses from the celebrated sea,
not these numbed-and-stunned fractions,
blue-hinged refugees, numbered survivors,
one for every two deceased,
without pride, without purse,
continental refuse of Poseidon's curse.

Beneath my heft of liberty,
they still appear homeless, tempest-tossed,
cataclysmically incomplete to me.

It is not nice to beguile the Mother of Exiles.
Grieved, I crack the light on this forlorn golden door.
My gift, my lamp moves along the paralytic shore.

from

Iowa: A Place to Poem

2012

Eastern Goldfinch

Mine, sweet thistle-bee
Gold-panned bird bricks memory
By the ounce, she wings

Old Geode

Bury me with old geode.
I, who tire of skipping along white man's road.
My wound is weathered from trying to prove—
White man, I cannot sell you what does not move.

Deposit me like lava-hardened seed—
Deep into the conscience of earth's cavity.
Water once, with insincere tears,
And I will crystallize the gesture for composite years.

For that will not be my stone upon your manifest street.
Mine is the shape of fury underneath your topsoil scheme.
What lies I endured for your destiny, what lies beneath—
Rocks the spirited soil and will rise in a dead man's dream.

Bury me with old geode.
What use is truce with frontier folk?
Your devil's dirt, my sacred residence—
So goes free soul to cryptic sediment.

Land Between Two Rivers

Like pillows and throws
between twisting bed posts,
this land between two rivers
comforts and climbs,
rises, resigns
in graceful reply
to the hand of the Giver.

Mesopotamia of the Midwest,
nation's most fertile crest,
your lush-and-green for eternity's keeping.
Protected you lie
among fields of sweeping lullabies
where only clouds serve as spy
to your resourceful sleeping.

Crinoid, Sea Lily

Alien of the deep,
the stone sea,
you rise with your orb,
your ghost machine.
The spells of dead goddesses
suspend like old vines
from your encrusted petals.
Whether you are eras or oceans away
from the rock-bottom beach
where you strayed—
it is no longer time's plate of debate
to settle.

Slain albatross for the dinosaur,
how could you lose
an entire Milky Way of water?
Which snarl, which scale
did you use to sign dry earth's
tablet treaty?

Or did you cry,
Seahorse, Seahorse!
My kingdom for a seahorse!

Be careful what you ask for, love.
The tide got out of town—
and left you,
Poseidon's ditched prototype
in a primitive enclave of concrete city.

December 28, 1846

Winter stars are first candles we see.
We guest homesteaders—
We children of the Territory.
Christmas, as our families attend it—
Three eves past.
We've boxing to do—colors and wraps.
Our men are in Mexico, guiding a war.
We've snow up to our souls;
And the knee shakes of more.
The year is about to take to sleigh,
Bids sleepy plows beneath—warm, idle night.
It leaves behind one last package—
Admission to the Union, to Iowans' delight.
The meadowlands are a white card;
We pioneer forms have our histories to inscribe:
Between observed birth of Our Savior
And fresh calendar's first day,
Iowa pushes the coldest of irons to become a state—
While the rest of the nation is on holiday.

Trappistine Nuns and Caramels, Our Lady of the Mississippi Abbey

Within this box
of assorted nuns,
I choose the creamy,
uncoated ones.
The kindest sweets
knelt in translucent wraps
who package themselves in prayer
and light-corn syrup saps.

I select the goodie-graces
that the Lord and FDA inspect—
who daily take ethereal exams,
then pass each strict and silent test.

I crave the penitent, saintly ones—
who fold their palms,
make sugar from sour—
who keep themselves for God
and hermit's hours.

I want the dulcet dames,
quiet as a napping tabby
who prowl their vespers
about the abbey—

the chosen hands
who craft afternoon candy
with the Creator's blessing
and inundating, sisterly loving—

To Darkness with dieting; I will take one dozen.

The Everly Brothers
After the duo's *Wake Up, Little Susie*

In backseat drama of dark alert,
Susie wakes to her Peyton Place.
She gathers seams of cockled poodle skirt.
Her saddle shoes gallop from disheveled waist.
A bobby sock brands her otherwise bare hip
while boyfriend plots parental script.

They will tell good folks the couple fell asleep under stars,
supple report, could happen to any set of kids.
Why, if only the Coupe were cooped with dependable alarm,
if only the FDA would approve a bottle of Enovid.
Burning broken rubber, the deuce heads out to sell the excuse-news,
to cover all four stolen bases, to minister to the morning bruise.

On her daddy's porch, rocks the knowing years,
with worry-red eyes and purse-bled lip.
He'll let them speak themselves to tears,
then roll out the usual chastening whip.
Yes, he will be the last to accept such a story styled.
He will be the first to spank his asleep-in-the-womb grandchild.

Marian the Librarian

Professor Harold Hill is in the business
of selling rigged instruments—
usurped uniforms, impalpable music lessons
no trumpet player can get a mouth around.

Unfortunately for our visiting con,
the library, or should one say,
the librarian is open,
open and wide-eyed
to the sting and harsh reflection
of his smoke and mirrors.

Prudent and sage
to Harry's chicanery game,
Marian the Librarian turns
a distrusting eye, cautious page
to Hill's unstable claims.

River City is a pool hall
swimming in sin.
Give the boys bugles!
Let the holy healing of the Heartland begin!

Marian intuits a fraud.
The good book pusher infers a wisp.
Until the loquacious professor
tutors her brother in overcoming his lisp.

Now, the librarian is in love with the lout.

The town's troubles are long-train gone.
Sound the 76 trombones!

You see, Marian the Librarian was long overdue to check out—
The heart is an instrument of its own.

Cloris Leachman as Ruth Popper, ***The Last Picture Show***

As she opens the porch door,
a laugh track from a studio audience
on the rabbit ears behind her
barrels through the disheveled hair,
foot dust and desperation of a lonely woman's
disbelieving eyes.

Without ducktail or luck, Sonny stands on the other side of welcome
and hops her for coffee.
Like a game-show contestant,
Ruth replies, *I guess.*

Blue wallpaper, freshly hung, endless hours ago, unglues.
She and her civics-lesson paramour walk their neglected souls into the kitchen.

Mrs. Popper apologizes to the boy.
The coach's wife is still in her bathrobe for afternoon soaps.
Her senses are shaking, unidentifiable, even to her.
The object of his angst-rejection,
she lets the saucer fly.

Cup of culpability and pot of joe, too, if it matters to you.
The steaming grounds land on the icebox to fume and cool.

It is the end of an era and error.

The lecture she spurns on that poor Crawford kid needs no note-taking.
This is after class; real-life teacher's turn to sass.
The rasp in her voice cannot pronounce any hard *g*'s
in *guilt* or *wrong* as in *I haven't done anything wron....*

Ruth pops him, *You're the one! You're the one who should be sorry!*
Angry in Anarene, she would have been dressed episodes ago
had he only continued to call and commit statutory acts.

Not even Cybill Shepherd as Jacy Farrow could breast such blame, withstand it.
Weeping cheek to cheek, the moment's sorrow unhands him.
It is royal theatre about to close.
Ruth rounds give-a-care's corner, rubs the boy's plaid collar.
Swept for dead, love or indifference, there, to reprimand him.
Her scarlet tongue speaks, without any hard *g*'s, only hard feelin's,
Never you mind—she throat-strokes, not for adultery, but silver-screen abandon.

Dan Gable

Like any wrestler at any level,
there is no substitute for me.
When I take my agenda to the mat,
no mate is on the sidelines
to assist, check, or screen.

Unlike any athlete I ever met,
advantage appeared to favor him,
the sinew in his shoulder,
the granite in his chin.

I followed blue-chip recruit from Waterloo,
trailed him all the way to Ames.
Nearly two-hundred bouts,
I dueled the boy, then man,
but could scarcely graze a leg.

He made mincemeat of me in Munich
despite my bond with the Soviets.
He made me grovel for
something silver,
submit to
something bronze—

another sober podium of regret.

Yes, I am jealous; I am sour
with every victory he ingested
triumphant and sweet.

He pinned a loser's laurel atop my shamed face,
forced me to spit out my bloody name.

Alas, I am Defeat.

Dewey Readmore Books
Spencer, Iowa

Winter is known for making its deposits—
record snowfall, against-the-grain wind, uncompromising cold.
So the 1988 season was perhaps overdue, late fees pending,
for the drop of a heartbreaker
in the shape of a kitty.
A harsh enough January in northwest Iowa
seizes all nine lives of a creature
before Cupid has chance to draw first arrow, first valentine.
Huddled in a corner, heartbeat down to the last decimal,
checked out—
Dewey Readmore Books was waiting for his new title.
Like Harold Hill in *The Music Man*,
the meager meow was waiting to be saved by the town librarian.
Vicki Myron was on her way.

Yes, Dewey was to become the latest edition,
permanent addition to the walls of the written.
Paw and pauper were welcome
among the stacks of books and literary crowd.
Like the stone lions of New York City Library,
Dewey stretched as sentry and night watchman.
He knew a good book. He knew a good reader.
In time, he welcomed in the DVD and easy-access computer.
In a small town legendary for its fires,
the orange tabby was a-blaze of fame—
county, state, nation, world.
He was a good scratch for the town.
But perhaps, most of all, he was a silent storyteller,
and the curious claw needed Miss Vicki to write them all down.

This is a rare collection of fur, courage, and care—
a bowl of gold disguised as a rib cage pinned in brisk metal—
the cat that came in from the cold—
nursed, no librarianed, back to life—
frisky and full of fine fettle.

—for Vicki Myron

Monet at Brucemore Gardens, Cedar Rapids

He has painted all of Europe,
last lily, known pond.
Great Atlantic has served its purpose
as parting, reflective bridge.
His penchant for flat-surfaces
carries him to where the Plains begin.
Here, the Cedar River breaks
among broken light and broken flowers.
The turrets and steep gables provide
precise divides of shade, seclusion, refuge
from fleeting season and hour.
The rose's hue must be subdued;
prairie orchid adrift in sudden water.
He acquaints with oil the coneflower's coil.
Haystacks brood,
just outside Outdoor Room,
but his brush with them on this continent—
not a trace.
Impressed with Iowa,
he spends agrarian days
knitting, framing Brucemore's bouquet
pieced and centered in Queen Anne's lace.

Maquoketa Caves

Given this dark mouth by God,
at last, I speak.
Old clothes, temporary dwellers, come, creep inside—
mind the limestone drapery.
Form one bandit-circle inside my black cathedral.
The only light I will ever see,
the flash-smile, upon your faces and eyes.

Tell me, shadow-visitors,
have you lit or leaned on my native son,
the fine and fleeted, feathered one?
He went to head raccoon
when my flowstone gathered young.
Night wings beat for his arrow-blood retreat on high.

A hollow soul like mine has room for faith to live.
For his return, my life's work churned this natural bridge.
A passage his skins had to cross but once, but never did.
My patient prayer balanced a rock to lookout-sit.
Into a search party of thirteen canyons, my private stones split.
Nothing found but robbers to steal my pearls
and seize the milkmoon from my stalactite sky.

A cave needs company
like the flooded crave rain.
Still, alabaster angels
invade, invade.

Here is a lunchbox the last field trip
forgot to claim.

God, I would put this mouth to final dusk
for silent chance to turn my cry-waters away.

Montauk, Governor Larrabee's Mansion, Clermont

Montauk in elegant estate, politely refuses her curtains.
Rail workers are laying tracks before the pines,
And she wants to see for certain
That Turkey River finds the shyest valley,
That good farmer's interest is served unhindered,
All fields have full lungs until grains
Separate from breath upon the garlands of winter.

In private library, Governor Larrabee seated at Wooten desk,
Inks an entreaty to Henderson, the future House Speaker.
He distrusts pursuits of smoke and station,
Motives of the locomotive,
Soot-stain on prairie fringe, boxcar-burden on bloodied nation
While Montauk seals the letter with Queen Victoria's stone.

Song soirees rise like warm bread from Juilliard-trained hardwoods.
Daily events discussed among sitting portraits at tea-cart time.
Coalport china waits for first course
As lawn generals and admiral statue look out across a miller's sky—
In case the South, under Reconstruction, decides again to rise.

Montauk in graced estate kindly refuses her curtains.
Lace trim and dress coats know the evening dinner ring,
But what main-course discourse will answer the Railroad Question?
There are winded children at her doorstep.
There is lazy marmalade rendered in Roman parlor.
There is a lady stone-stepping from a carriage
To take a clay mason's hand in honor
While Montauk serves as Algonquin lighthouse, turn-of-century mirror.

Porch roses and Brown Swiss cattle keep her unlikely company.
Thorn, brick, and bovine call the mansion mine.
Heirloom hills are filled with music from below town's pipe organ.
The entire countryside in a corset-bind,
For, like the railroad, Montauk has her ties.

Miss Havisham in the Meadows

This is the release I wanted—
the decaying mansion, the stillborn marriage—
at last, both institutions set me free.

Nothing in Satis House has satisfied.
Even the cliché fog of London lifts
like the hand of a porter accepting a continental pass.

A new woman needs a new world,
the meadows of America,
rising as fine stalk to face a sun-dripped future—
in lieu of the marshes unsteadying the past.

But, Pip, the damned wedding gown—
            follows me here—

the fluff-fuzz of an early dandelion,
            the veils of white violets,
                      a skein of prairie clover.

I wear them as the soil wears in the wind.

Between two rivers, I see that I am only between tears.

Nothing here has moved beyond heartbreak.

Again, I am left at the tattered altar of my soul—
explaining to a dark minister the great flat lands—

I have come to expect.

                      After Dickens' *Great Expectations*

Medusa at Gay Pride,
East Village, Des Moines

I had come to a parade,
entries of fag-force, sheer gay power
with streams of flaming tissue paper—
and a closeted farmer's***donated barbed wire***.

With fierce hair and criminal lipstick,
I blended like sweetened tequila with these summer queens,
serpents flying from my ferocious hair,
serpents of their own unleashed in cut-off leather jeans.

I had come in the guise of a friend;
only a cauldron of coals below knows my true intent to disparage
their knee-high boots stomping for civil rights,
their hissy-hollers celebrating a god's changed mind on marriage.

It is too soon to show them my eyes,
so I groove like Madonna atop a float's feathered chassis.
In time, every bump-and-grind hind will be mine
when I mix witchcraft with rainbow confetti.

The event starts fifty minutes late.
Isn't that just like the gays?
And they wonder why supreme justice
ever made their tootsie-tushes wait.

At last, the entourage sashays into Grand Avenue.
My hissing crown rides a hate-crime throne.
The street stuff turns to wave at me, Hell's homophobe.
I turn to stare, hangs the air, as all turns to stone.

The Cricket Waltz, Surf Ballroom, Clear Lake

The crickets hum, the crickets show
to string their hymns, summer's repose.
June surf is high; ballroom, bloom-filled,
two turns away from winter's mill.

The crickets rub their oiled limbs
to court hardwood with violins.
Buddy on stage to hound his hits
beneath warm moon, beneath horned rims.

The crickets' song—before its time.
Holly, wreath-hung, foretells dark eyes.
Cold waltz of four,
frozen ruins.

Our Lady of the Lake sets sail
to bruise.

If you believe in dance parties,
by call season or cloud machine…

an aircraft lifts, memorial gifts

field the fall.

Mother Goose at Fejervary Park Children's Zoo, Davenport

Next time you're there, tipping into the petting zoo,
notice her paralyzed presence among runaway leaves.

She is shocked the children, the characters she groomed,
would take their pies, sheep, spiders, horns—leave her to grief.

Those wired spectacles cannot make-believe her mind.
She gave her young legend, climax, happy endings, shoes.

Still, it sounds to her—their contrary goodbyes, quite unkind.
With time on down feathers, what else is an empty nest to do?

The passageway through her breast, to her heart, is cupboard bare.
Her white frame bumps at goose thought of kids who visit-enter.

Blue as the flop-hat that tops her statuesque air,
Mother Goose parks and pines in shade of everyday winter.

Left wing of longing, right of recluse—in granny tandem.
Nothing but rhyme on her hands to nurse her through hurt of abandon.

The Little Mermaid, Statue and Fountain, Kimballton
Spenserian Sonnet

Atop a prairie stone, water mocks her.
Aqua-everywhere, not a spurt to swim.
Such the sacrifice of Triton's daughter,
for mortal legs, a dream's sensible limbs.

Recast bronze, she leans toward Copenhagen.
Recast by Disney, film-fictive princess.
Throned-alone with regret's glare, rebirth fins,
she assumes her fate: Mermaid of the Midwest.

No pleasure pining, no treasure on breast,
all senses, speechless, reflect on pout lips.
Replica-sea, leaf-green, King Corn's conquest.
Hope is anchored without romance or ships.

The toll for human soul, stroll distracts her.
Prince Charming is a chore on a tractor.

The Butter Cow, Iowa State Fair

We come in from the jip-stand heat
to watch her humble graze in the crafted cold.
Indeed, she is a constant star in the East,
east side of Des Moines, throned, a century old.
She has answered to the hands of four sculptors
who with wood, wire, metal and steel-mesh frame—
add 600 pounds of low-moisture butter
to give her dimension, legacy, and fame.

Each year, in line, distanced by glass, we pass her stately yoke
and guest sidekicks—astronaut, gymnast, rock-n-roll paragons.
We offer gifts of wonder, amazement, corn-dog-on-a-stick
to cast on her coat the color of cornsilk, cosmic, or chiffon.

Once little churns at her hooves, our chore boots now stride by her ribs of cream.
Roll out the yellow carpet. She is our Elizabeth, if Iowa, indeed, has a queen.

—for Norma "Duffy" Lyon

Floyd of Rosedale

Ah, pig, the Kinnick crowd of November
wiggles into their blankets of black and gold, Hawkeye Nation.
Gophers in town, front-bucked teeth to dismember.
Backlit by tuba-brass pep band, you stand, at your sideline station.

We've missed you, pig. Since last drift of leaves
you've been penned up in St. Paul—a captive, refugee, visitor—
swine stolen by touchdowns, thieving referees.
To bask in your autumnal bronze, hog, our squad will bruise and blister.

Born live in 1935, our Rosedale, your home,
your cast-fat symbolizes fight on the field, trough-trophy victor,
first set on a governors' bet and ignited by racial overtones,
when the Ebony Eel battered by a white tide of unsportsmanlike hitters.

Wilbur, Arnold, Babe—their grunts, too, know fame.
Doubt those snouts can be the star-lard in their own pigskin game.

Rockford Sock Mittens

The poorest girls
seem to possess the richest memories.

Take, my mother, for instance—
she had all the demographics
stacked against her
like a tall drift of blizzard against the barn:

The Great Depression,
small-farm folk in southern Iowa,
one-room schoolhouse,
single pair of shoes for the winter,
single pair of mittens for life.

She lost those hand warmers,
somewhere between number-figuring and flirting;
retail replacement was out of the question.

Like FDR, her mother made her a New Deal:

a second pair cut
from Dad's work-worn Rockford socks—
freckled gray, red-nosed at the heel,
snow-capped around the calf.
The feet were worn out, but the tops were still good.

The footwear was molded into finger furnaces, overnight.

How proud she was to show them, even to the snooty girls,
their pleated noses boarding the pulsing bus.

Shouldn't the poor girl be saddened by the privileged laughs—
shouldn't little Marjorie hide the makeshift footings
from the mocks that leave a heart in need of darning?

Why, no! replied her discovery eyes.
Upon my palms, I can feel my father farming.

—for Marjorie Thompson
who has lived a glorious life
in a glorious coat of many colors—

The Newspaper Iowa Depends Upon

If you're a lifelong Iowan,
or ever found yourself on the doorstep
of an Iowa home, any given morning,
then you know it is more than a mere
paper in a puddle.

The *Des Moines Register* arrives
each sunrise
with the daily trace
of our recent lives.

Banded, bound, and bundled,
book of acts, edition of human exchange,
rooster with a roster of print
to crow over the plains.

Familiar to farm and town,
no stranger to the Pulitzer,
it unfolds, unfolds
all the stories of our state and beyond
to be told.

I wish I were a dog,
so then from sidewalk to slipper,
I'd fetch it.

Reliable read,
along with my breakfast bread,
I bless it.

Van Allen Belts
THE IOWA AWARD COLLECTION

The sun god, Apollo, placed us here
to protect his mortal home.

It was an act of gratitude,
a protean promise to the vulnerable
that we, his shields, would morph
into whatever shape necessary
to guard against the onslaughts in orbit.

True. The heavens possess their fires,
just as the world radiates its liars.

But the moon was no hoax.
Astronauts arrived there,
walked the tranquil seas.

Belts conduct and prohibit.
Did it ever cross your scientific minds,
your disbelieving guises
that we allowed slipknots for clear passage?

Every day, you are touched by a fierce star
that could kill you in a strike.
Yet, without fear, suspicion, you accept its light.

Apollo was the first poet.
It moved him that humans longed for the moon.
He opened us, briefly, wider than a Mancini mile,

and the spacecrafts crossed through us safely,
and in style.

The Apostle of Wheat
THE IOWA AWARD COLLECTION

The apostle of wheat scribes in the field.
With ignorant hunger, he'd like to have a word—
You cannot have peace on an empty stomach.
The message catches wind, satiates the world.

Grain is in a green race with infants born.
Both bobbings lean forward, toward a global crawl.
If the booming population wins at the finish,
It is starvation, devastation—for all.

The apostle of wheat skips his own supper.
Big eyes, bloated bellies force him to work late.
Cresco, Calcutta know: Famine has the munchies.
It wants human need on a silver plate.

—In honor of Norman Borlaug, 1914-2009

Robert D. Ray,
Governor of Iowa, 1969-1983
THE IOWA AWARD COLLETION

He is the Iowa icon of the 1970s
like the have-a-nice-day smile,
pet rocks, shag carpeting, and disco.
It was tall-corn time, a slogan-to-live-by;
Iowa was a place to grow.
We saved our pop bottles for rainy-day nickels,
gave Southeast Asian refugees a home.

The first family of Iowa
inhabited the Victorian rooms
of elegant Terrace Hill for the first time.
And, we children of the state,
thrived in safe keeping—
through the media vines of Vietnam,
the summer of surprise when a president resigned.

That was then, those 70s trends,
like youth and yo-yos—
break their strings and roll
their bones, their bodies away.

I hear he is a photographer now.
And I imagine his silhouette in a stately frame—
Standing over the Native American burial grounds
He dignified
With proper graves.

I hummed for Governor Ray. I cheered for him.
I knew nothing of campaigns.
Something just rang true-blue to me
When the ad jingle advised—
Let a leader lead the way.

American Gothic House, Eldon
THE IOWA AWARD COLLECTION

Quietly, a drifter trips to my yard,
Entranced as if in requisite study.
He calls me backdrop, and it settles hard.
His brush of air, annoys and disturbs me.

Round of spectacles and round at mid-waist,
This Wood-be painter asks for my porch-profile.
I may be the house, but he is fresh paint
To ask that I turn my gables, effect a smile.

You'll need frown's farmer, and you'll need stern's wife.
I advise with my south eye window-arching.
And it's best to depict me in dust-white
To convince of regionalism's aching.

His masterpiece eyes spy a rarity.
I bring'm to size. *Wait for the parodies!*

Hoover Birthplace, August 10, 1874, West Branch
NATIONAL HISTORIC LANDMARKS OF IOWA

A plague of grasshoppers misses
eastern Iowa by a meadow.

Inside a two-room cottage,
a woman forges a newborn.

The smithy cools its smoke
amidst silver, summer heat.

It's a boy,
so a bluestem crochets outside the window.

In the next room,
water knits its way to steam.

The grown bones don't mind,
but the baby begins to rattle.

In the next century,
a plague of hard times will not miss this child.

In an oval room,
he will forge swarms of policy and remedy.

The public will not cool its smoke;
he delivers one term.

He has missed his mother—
and the meadow.

Trees of Marcourt Lane

Like late autumn air,
the Sunday edition on my lawn, crisp and clean,
The Newspaper Iowa Depends On, delivered right on time.
Among raked traces of summer, not a scent of evil emits
from the folded market page, not a bullish sign—
but it won't compensate for the bound one, ever late,
the missing issue that occupies my mind—
stuck in brain-bushes that September morning
when my newsboy stole his own headlines.

I do believe in witness trees,
the truth within these limbs of Marcourt Lane.
You, tree, the origin of paper, don't your wooded rings bear some root of annual blame?
He was last seen here—boy, bundle, and wagon—surely—
some of your branches were breakfast-awake,
to see the wicked wheel, abduction, routing down our street,
to see a boy throwing print for dimes,
and a car or van, waiting, fuming for the vicious take.

Bag—abandoned, curbside—
Where were you, shelter? What of you, shade?
Untrunk your memory. Were you a pile of nervous leaves afraid?
Kid carrier may be alive, but he won't shake a stick at seventh grade.
Do your crowns ever wonder how his mother observes the ache of Labor Day?

Good trees, it's inane to think you'd ever speak to the West Des Moines Police,
but if I watered you from a milk carton with the child's school picture,
would the solution become elementary?
Would you tell your forest-story, secretly, to me?
Would your pulp fingers point the way to any leads?
Your arbor must harbor some reminiscent mist of the disappeared in grief.
Why, then, in spring, do you bloom and hang in such lovely green and white wreaths?

Paper birch, purge. Dogwood, bark. Let me hear your sylvan song.
Ash exasperated—scarcely a leaf of hope hangs on—
Just an early winter buyer-and-seller's wind,
blowing old smoke over silent wood's auction block—
bringing down Yuppie Town, as the neighborhood's good-day bidding heart
breaks with another grievous dawn.
The search party has to flee the scene—word is—fresh pot of coffee, elsewhere, is on—
Johnny Gosch, going once, Eugene Martin, going twice—
the last innocent kid's flick—as the Register frees from his wrist—

going gone.   *-for Johnny Gosch & Eugene Martin*
                                Des Moines Register carriers, abducted, 1982, 1984

Provender
Dry grain, fodder for livestock

Pilgrims of the prairie,
each with a girth of three ships,
the livestock gather with bowed skulls,
ruminate their lumbering prayers before the founding rock of grain tables.

Their voyage is one of storage.

It is a christened calling of the blessed corn-fed
to crack the yielded berries, partake of the by-the-bushel bird,
treat themselves to the time-share trough.

Farmer Profit looks over the horns of plenty—
       feeding off the fat-Atlantic of the land—
              to become the fat of the land.

Beneath the heft of hooves,
November's plain spreads its ocean-cloth of amber waves.

A majesty of purple mountains to the west
overlooks the fodder-feast and reigns as lot-tombs of lavender.

In town, the butcher behind chilled glass, awaits, the after-graze
with white wraps of surrender.

Amidst the silo's storm,
the cattle are coming. The cattle are coming—yonder.
Look at their Plymouth snouts,
their thrash-waving tongues—lapping the salt-licked trails

of provender.

Native Prairie Fragment

The final shards of light are knives.
After centuries of broken shock,
the terrace-tiling machines seize even these.
Glints of sweat off the plowshare,
progressives tilling the prairie's last one-tenth
of one percent—
for their wind power generators, solar-powered stores.

      The last pale coneflower reverses its rays
          in exchange for development's luminous coin—
an entire ecosystem recedes
      for the cost of first and last month's rent—

Once, the fields heard talk of *flower power*,
and the sweet blue aster came out from hiding.
But, they plucked it and placed it in a girl's hair,
shoved daisies down gun shafts—

Stripped down to a strip mall,
the last lone acre of prickly sea
ebbs beneath a navigating sky and cries—
What for?

The *buzzword* is that the native prairie has stopped *buzzing*.
Buzzing chains under warranty to silence the wings.
They need land, you understand—even the environmental humans—
those cycle-conscious things—

The green remaining in the native blade is jaded—
retracting like a farewell tide to a tractor's tire and traction—

and even that will be contracted out in fractions.

EPILOGUE POEM

A Bluebird in Winter
State Bird of Missouri

Like winter,
the bluebird takes the tree,
bereft of its leaves.

Its arrival,
a kind of departure.

Poet Robert Frost had the message right,
but the color wrong.
Nothing this blue can stay.

Like the soul,
you want it to fly—

but not fly away.

ABOUT THE AUTHOR

John D. Thompson is the author of 9 books of poetry including
Iowa: A Place to Poem, Tender Revolutions,
99 Voices, 99 Lives: County Poems of Iowa,
On Holiday, and
Titanic: A Centenarian Voyage in Verse.
A United States Senate Scholar and member of
American MENSA, Thompson holds an
MFA in Creative Writing/Poetry from New England College.
He has completed post-graduate coursework in poetry
at the Harvard University Creative Writing Program
and University of Iowa Writers' Workshop,
both with honors.
Thompson has served as adjunct faculty at
Des Moines Area Community College and
Indian Hills Community College in Iowa.
He currently lives in Pella, Iowa,
and teaches at Eddyville-Blakesburg-Fremont CSD.
Thompson is a member of the Iowa Poetry Association.

The author is available for appearances.
Contact **statepoetpro@yahoo.com**

Love Letter from Luxembourg

www.ingramcontent.com/pod-product-compliance
Lightning Source LLC
Chambersburg PA
CBHW080335170426
43194CB00014B/2576